Introduction

Why This Book?

- ➢ The evolving role of procureme... ... ...
- ➢ The difference between tactical and strategic procurement.
- ➢ The importance of becoming a strategic procurement manager in today's business environment.

Who Is This Book For?

- ➢ Procurement managers looking to elevate their careers.
- ➢ Professionals aspiring to transition into strategic roles.
- ➢ Organizations seeking to build a strategic procurement function.

What You Will Learn

- ➢ Key skills, mindset shifts, and strategies to become a strategic procurement manager.
- ➢ Real-world examples, case studies, and actionable steps.

Part 1: Understanding the Foundations

The Role of a Procurement Manager

1) Traditional responsibilities: sourcing, purchasing, and supplier management.
2) The limitations of a tactical approach.

What Is Strategic Procurement?

3) Definition and key principles.
4) How strategic procurement adds value to the organization.
5) The shift from cost-saving to value creation.

The Strategic Procurement Manager's Mindset

6) Thinking beyond transactions.
7) Embracing innovation, collaboration, and long-term planning.
8) Becoming a business partner rather than a support function.

Part 2: Building the Skillset

Core Competencies of a Strategic Procurement Manager

9) Analytical thinking and data-driven decision-making.
10) Negotiation and relationship management.
11) Risk management and mitigation.
12) Financial acumen and understanding of total cost of ownership (TCO).

Mastering Procurement Technology

13) Leveraging procurement software and tools (e.g., ERP, e-procurement, spend analytics).
14) The role of AI, machine learning, and automation in procurement.

Developing Leadership and Influence

15) Leading cross-functional teams.
16) Influencing stakeholders and gaining executive buy-in.
17) Building a culture of strategic thinking within the procurement team.

Part 3: Implementing Strategic Procurement Practices

Strategic Sourcing

18) Category management and segmentation.
19) Supplier relationship management (SRM) and collaboration.
20) Sustainable and ethical sourcing practices.

Driving Innovation Through Procurement

21) Identifying opportunities for innovation in the supply chain.
22) Partnering with suppliers to co-create value.
23) Leveraging market trends and disruptions.

Risk Management and Resilience

24) Identifying and mitigating supply chain risks.
25) Building a resilient procurement strategy.
26) Scenario planning and contingency strategies.

Measuring and Communicating Value

27) Key performance indicators (KPIs) for strategic procurement.
28) Demonstrating ROI and value creation to stakeholders.
29) Continuous improvement and benchmarking.

Part 4: Navigating the Transition

From Tactical to Strategic: A Step-by-Step Guide

30) Assessing your current role and identifying gaps.
31) Creating a personal development plan.
32) Building a roadmap for your transition.

Overcoming Common Challenges

33) Resistance to change within the organization.
34) Balancing tactical responsibilities with strategic initiatives.
35) Managing time and priorities effectively.

36) **Case Studies and Success Stories**
37) Real-world examples of procurement managers who made the transition.

Appendices

Appendix A: Tools and Resources for Procurement Professionals

✓ Recommended books, courses, and certifications.
✓ List of procurement software and platforms.

Appendix B: Templates and Frameworks

✓ Strategic sourcing templates.
✓ Supplier evaluation scorecards.
✓ Risk assessment frameworks.

Appendix C: Glossary of Procurement Terms

✓ Key terms and definitions for quick reference.

Introduction

Why This Book?

Procurement has long been viewed as a necessary function within organizations, responsible for sourcing goods and services at the best price. Traditionally, procurement was seen as a tactical, back-office activity focused on reducing costs, managing suppliers, and ensuring timely delivery of materials. However, in today's rapidly changing business environment, procurement has evolved into a strategic function that directly impacts an organization's profitability, competitiveness, and long-term success.

Modern procurement professionals are no longer just buyers; they are strategic partners who contribute to business growth, risk management, and innovation. The shift from tactical to strategic procurement is not just about improving efficiency—it is about creating value. Organizations that embrace strategic procurement gain a competitive edge by fostering stronger supplier relationships, optimizing supply chains, and making data-driven decisions that align with corporate goals.

This book is designed to help procurement professionals understand this transformation and position themselves as strategic leaders within their organizations. It will guide you through the essential mindset shifts, skills, and methodologies required to master strategic procurement and move beyond the traditional cost-cutting approach.

The Difference Between Tactical and Strategic Procurement

To understand why the shift from tactical to strategic procurement is critical, it is essential to recognize the key differences between the two approaches:

Tactical Procurement focuses on short-term needs, transactional activities, and cost reduction. It involves reacting to immediate procurement requirements, negotiating contracts based on price alone, and managing suppliers at an operational level.

Strategic Procurement takes a long-term, proactive approach. It aligns procurement activities with the organization's overall business strategy, emphasizes value creation rather than just cost-cutting, and fosters strong supplier partnerships that drive innovation and competitive advantage.

Some key aspects that differentiate strategic procurement from tactical procurement include:

Aspect	Tactical Procurement	Strategic Procurement
Focus	Cost reduction, transactional efficiency	Value creation, business alignment
Approach	Reactive, short-term planning	Proactive, long-term planning
Supplier Relationships	Adversarial, price-driven	Collaborative, innovation-driven
Decision-Making	Based on price and immediate needs	Based on total cost of ownership (TCO) and strategic value
Technology Use	Limited, manual processes	Leverages automation, AI, and analytics

The transition from tactical to strategic procurement is not just a change in processes but a fundamental shift in thinking. Procurement managers who adopt a strategic mindset will position themselves as essential contributors to their organization's success.

The Importance of Becoming a Strategic Procurement Manager

Organizations today operate in an increasingly complex and volatile global market. Supply chain disruptions, regulatory changes, sustainability demands, and technological advancements have made procurement more challenging than ever. In this environment, a purely tactical approach to procurement is no longer sufficient.

Strategic procurement managers play a crucial role in:

> **Driving Business Growth** – By aligning procurement strategies with corporate objectives, they help organizations reduce risk, improve efficiency, and capitalize on market opportunities.

> **Enhancing Supplier Collaboration** – Strong relationships with suppliers lead to better pricing, improved service levels, and access to innovation.

> **Managing Risk** – Strategic procurement helps identify potential supply chain risks and implement mitigation strategies to ensure business continuity.

> **Promoting Sustainability and Ethical Sourcing** – Organizations are increasingly being held accountable for their environmental and social impact. A strategic procurement manager ensures ethical sourcing practices and promotes sustainability initiative

> **Leveraging Technology and Data** – Digital transformation is reshaping procurement. Strategic procurement professionals

use data analytics, AI, and automation to optimize decision-making and improve efficiency.

As procurement continues to gain strategic importance, professionals who can adapt to this evolving landscape will be in high demand. This book provides the knowledge and tools needed to make that transition successfully.

Who Is This Book For?

This book is designed for professionals at different stages of their procurement careers who aspire to enhance their strategic capabilities. Whether you are an experienced procurement manager, a professional looking to transition into procurement, or an organization seeking to improve its procurement function, this book offers valuable insights and practical guidance.

Procurement Managers Looking to Elevate Their Careers

If you are already working in procurement and want to move beyond transactional activities, this book will help you develop the skills and strategic mindset needed to take on leadership roles. You will learn how to shift from cost-cutting to value creation, build strong supplier partnerships, and leverage technology to enhance procurement efficiency.

Professionals Aspiring to Transition into Strategic Roles

Many professionals in supply chain management, finance, operations, and other business functions are interested in moving into strategic procurement. This book provides a comprehensive roadmap for understanding the fundamental principles of procurement and developing the competencies required to succeed in a strategic role.

Organizations Seeking to Build a Strategic Procurement Function

Companies that rely on procurement as a competitive advantage will benefit from implementing strategic procurement practices. Whether you are a business leader, C-level executive, or procurement director, this book will help you transform your procurement function into a key driver of business success. You will gain insights into best practices, case studies, and frameworks that can be applied to build a high-performing procurement team.

What You Will Learn

This book is structured to provide a step-by-step guide to mastering strategic procurement. It is packed with real-world examples, case studies, and actionable steps that will enable you to implement strategic procurement practices effectively.

By reading this book, you will learn:

Key Skills and Mindset Shifts

> How to transition from a tactical to a strategic procurement approach.

> The importance of data-driven decision-making in procurement.

> How to develop strong supplier relationships and foster collaboration.

> The role of leadership and influence in procurement management.

Strategies for Strategic Procurement Management

> Implementing category management and supplier segmentation.

Developing and executing a strategic sourcing strategy.

Managing procurement risks and ensuring supply chain resilience.

Leveraging procurement technology, automation, and AI.

Real-World Case Studies and Examples

Throughout the book, you will find case studies from leading organizations that have successfully implemented strategic procurement. These examples will provide practical insights into how companies have navigated procurement challenges and transformed their operations.

Actionable Steps to Implement Strategic Procurement

Each chapter will include practical exercises, templates, and checklists to help you apply the concepts learned. By the end of this book, you will have a clear action plan for implementing strategic procurement within your organization.

Part 1: Understanding the Foundations

The Role of a Procurement Manager

Procurement managers have long been the backbone of organizational operations. Traditionally, their responsibilities have centered around ensuring that goods and services are acquired at the best possible prices, on time, and in accordance with contractual terms. This role, deeply rooted in tactical activities, involves tasks such as sourcing, purchasing, and supplier management. However, as global markets evolve and the dynamics of supply chains become more complex, the traditional role is rapidly transforming. In this chapter, we explore the foundational aspects of procurement management, delve into its traditional responsibilities, and critically examine the limitations of a purely tactical approach.

Traditional Responsibilities: Sourcing, Purchasing, and Supplier Management

Sourcing

At the heart of procurement lies sourcing. Sourcing is the process of identifying potential suppliers who can provide the goods or services that an organization requires. Traditionally, sourcing has involved:

> **Market Research:** Procurement managers conduct extensive market research to identify suppliers who can meet the organization's needs. This includes analyzing supplier capabilities, quality standards, delivery times, and reliability.

> **Supplier Evaluation:** Once potential suppliers are identified, the next step is evaluation. Managers compare suppliers based on various criteria such as cost, quality, capacity, and reputation. The evaluation process often includes requests for proposals (RFPs) and supplier audits.

Negotiation: After narrowing down potential suppliers, procurement managers negotiate contracts to secure favorable terms. Negotiation focuses on pricing, delivery schedules, payment terms, and after-sales support. The primary objective is to ensure that the supplier relationship is both beneficial and sustainable.

The sourcing process is critical as it lays the groundwork for a stable supply chain. Effective sourcing ensures that the organization has access to quality products at competitive prices, which is essential for maintaining operational efficiency and cost control.

Purchasing

Purchasing is the execution phase where the actual transaction occurs. It involves the formal process of ordering, receiving, and processing goods and services. Key elements of purchasing include:

Order Placement: Once a supplier is selected and a contract is negotiated, the procurement manager places orders. This process includes specifying quantities, delivery dates, and any other requirements stipulated in the contract.

Order Tracking: Procurement managers must monitor the progress of orders to ensure they are delivered on time. This often involves coordinating with logistics, warehousing, and production teams.

Invoice Processing and Payment: The purchasing function also covers the financial aspects, ensuring that invoices are accurate and payments are made promptly. This step is crucial for maintaining a good relationship with suppliers and securing favorable terms in future negotiations.

Purchasing, while seemingly straightforward, is a complex process that requires attention to detail and coordination across various departments. Even minor errors in this stage can lead to significant operational disruptions, highlighting the importance of precision and accountability in purchasing activities.

Supplier Management

Supplier management is the process of maintaining and nurturing relationships with suppliers to ensure ongoing collaboration and performance. Traditionally, this has involved:

> **Performance Monitoring:** Procurement managers regularly review supplier performance against contractual obligations. This includes evaluating quality, delivery times, and overall reliability.

> **Issue Resolution:** When problems arise, such as delays or quality issues, the procurement manager is responsible for addressing them swiftly. This may involve renegotiating terms, facilitating communication between internal stakeholders and suppliers, or even finding alternative sources.

> **Relationship Building:** Beyond transactional interactions, supplier management has a relational aspect. Long-standing relationships built on trust and mutual benefit can lead to more favorable terms, priority service, and innovative collaborations.

Effective supplier management is essential for minimizing risks associated with supply chain disruptions. It also helps organizations respond swiftly to changes in market conditions or shifts in demand, ensuring that production and service delivery remain uninterrupted.

The Limitations of a Tactical Approach

While traditional procurement responsibilities are essential, relying solely on tactical methods presents significant limitations. A tactical approach, which emphasizes short-term objectives such as cost reduction and efficient transaction processing, can undermine long-term strategic goals. In today's fast-paced and increasingly interconnected business environment, a purely tactical mindset can be detrimental to an organization's growth and resilience. Below, we examine several key limitations of the tactical approach.

Narrow Focus on Cost-Cutting

One of the primary criticisms of a tactical procurement approach is its narrow focus on cost reduction. While controlling costs is undeniably important, an overemphasis on short-term savings can lead to several issues:

Quality Compromises: In the race to secure the lowest price, organizations may inadvertently choose suppliers that do not meet quality standards. This can result in increased returns, production delays, and reputational damage.

Short-Term Gains, Long-Term Losses: Tactical cost-cutting measures may provide immediate financial relief, but they often ignore the broader implications for innovation, supplier loyalty, and market competitiveness. In the long run, the failure to invest in quality and strategic partnerships can erode competitive advantage.

Missed Opportunities for Value Creation: A singular focus on cost reduction can blind organizations to opportunities for value creation through collaboration, innovation, and continuous improvement. Strategic procurement, by contrast, seeks to balance cost with value, ensuring that savings are achieved without sacrificing long-term benefits.

Reactive rather than Proactive Management

A tactical approach tends to be reactive. Procurement managers operating tactically often respond to immediate needs or crises rather than anticipating future trends and challenges. This reactive stance has several drawbacks:

Inability to Anticipate Market Changes: By focusing solely on current transactions, tactical procurement managers may fail to foresee shifts in the market. Economic downturns, supply chain disruptions, or sudden changes in demand can catch organizations unprepared.

Limited Risk Mitigation: A reactive approach does not provide the necessary foresight to develop robust risk management strategies. Without proactive planning, organizations are more vulnerable to disruptions caused by geopolitical events, natural disasters, or shifts in regulatory landscapes.

Reduced Innovation: Reactive procurement often means sticking to established suppliers and conventional methods. This limits the opportunities for innovation that come from exploring new partnerships, adopting advanced technologies, or rethinking traditional procurement processes.

Lack of Alignment with Organizational Strategy

Procurement does not operate in a vacuum. Its activities should be aligned with the overall strategic objectives of the organization. However, tactical procurement often operates independently of the broader business strategy, leading to several challenges:

Siloed Operations: When procurement functions are isolated from other business units, there is little coordination with strategic planning. This siloed approach can lead to misaligned priorities, where procurement decisions are made without considering the organization's long-term goals.

Underutilization of Data: In many traditional setups, procurement decisions are made based on historical data or intuition rather than forward-looking analytics. This underutilization of data limits the ability to make informed decisions that align with market trends and strategic objectives.

Missed Collaboration Opportunities: A lack of strategic alignment often means that procurement is seen as a support function rather than a partner in strategic decision-making. This diminishes the influence of procurement managers in shaping overall business strategy and undermines the potential for cross-functional collaboration.

Inadequate Supplier Relationships

The tactical approach to procurement is typically transactional. Relationships with suppliers are viewed primarily through the lens of negotiation and cost. This perspective can hinder the development of deeper, more collaborative relationships that are essential for strategic success:

Transactional Interactions: When supplier relationships are based solely on transactions, there is little incentive for suppliers to invest in innovation or long-term improvements. The focus on price rather than value can lead to a lack of commitment from both parties.

Limited Information Sharing: Strategic procurement relies on open and transparent communication with suppliers to drive innovation and continuous improvement. Tactical approaches, however, tend to restrict the flow of information, preventing the kind of collaborative problem-solving that benefits both the organization and its suppliers.

Missed Opportunities for Joint Innovation: In today's competitive environment, many breakthroughs in product development, process improvement, and market expansion come from collaborative efforts between companies and their suppliers. A purely transactional relationship leaves little room for such joint initiatives, stifling creativity and innovation.

Challenges in Leveraging Technology and Data

The rapid pace of technological advancement is reshaping how procurement is conducted. Digital tools and data analytics can significantly enhance procurement processes by providing real-time insights and automating routine tasks. However, a tactical approach often fails to harness these benefits:

Underutilization of Digital Tools: Many traditional procurement setups rely on outdated systems and manual processes, which are not designed to integrate with modern digital solutions. This underutilization hampers efficiency and prevents procurement managers from gaining a competitive edge.

Data Silos and Inaccuracies: Tactical procurement frequently involves disparate systems that do not communicate with each other. The resulting data silos can lead to inaccuracies and a lack of a comprehensive view of procurement activities, hindering strategic decision-making.

Reactive Data Usage: Instead of using data to anticipate trends and optimize supplier relationships, tactical procurement often involves using data only to address immediate issues. This reactive data usage limits the ability to develop forward-looking strategies that can preempt problems and seize emerging opportunities.

Moving Beyond the Tactical: The Need for a Strategic Perspective

Recognizing the limitations of a purely tactical approach is the first step toward transforming procurement into a strategic function. By moving beyond short-term, cost-focused methods, procurement managers can unlock a range of benefits that contribute to overall business success. Here are some key elements that illustrate why a strategic perspective is crucial:

22

Embracing a Value-Creation Mindset

A strategic procurement manager focuses not only on reducing costs but also on creating value. This involves:

Holistic Decision-Making: Instead of evaluating suppliers solely based on price, managers consider total cost of ownership (TCO), which includes factors like quality, delivery reliability, and after-sales support.

Long-Term Partnerships: Developing relationships that foster collaboration, innovation, and continuous improvement can lead to better pricing, shared risk, and enhanced market competitiveness.

Innovation as a Driver: By partnering with suppliers in innovation initiatives, organizations can leverage new technologies, streamline processes, and create products that better meet market demands.

Proactive Risk Management and Resilience

Strategic procurement managers adopt a proactive approach to risk management. This involves:

Anticipating Disruptions: Using data analytics and market intelligence to identify potential risks—be it geopolitical shifts, natural disasters, or sudden changes in market demand—helps in developing contingency plans.

Scenario Planning: Engaging in scenario planning enables organizations to prepare for various outcomes. By modeling different scenarios, procurement teams can implement robust risk mitigation strategies and ensure business continuity even during turbulent times.

23

Diversification of Suppliers: Rather than relying on a single supplier, a strategic approach often involves diversifying the supplier base to mitigate risks. This diversification not only secures supply but also encourages competitive pricing and innovation.

Alignment with Organizational Strategy

When procurement is aligned with broader business goals, its impact is magnified. Strategic procurement managers work closely with other business units to ensure:

Cross-Functional Collaboration: By partnering with departments such as finance, operations, and R&D, procurement can ensure that sourcing decisions support overall strategic objectives.

Data-Driven Strategy: Leveraging advanced analytics and digital tools, procurement managers can forecast trends, identify opportunities for cost savings, and make decisions that are both informed and strategically aligned.

Sustainable Practices: In an era where sustainability and corporate social responsibility are paramount, strategic procurement integrates these values into its practices. This might include choosing suppliers who adhere to environmental standards, ethical labor practices, and social responsibility initiatives.

Leveraging Technology for Competitive Advantage

Modern procurement is at the intersection of technology and business strategy. By embracing digital transformation, procurement managers can:

Automate Routine Tasks: Automation reduces the time spent on transactional activities, allowing managers to focus on strategic initiatives.

Gain Real-Time Insights: Advanced analytics and integrated ERP systems provide real-time data that can be used to optimize procurement decisions, manage supplier performance, and forecast market trends.

Enhance Collaboration: Cloud-based platforms and digital communication tools facilitate better coordination between procurement teams, suppliers, and other stakeholders, leading to more agile and responsive supply chain management.

Case Example: Transforming Procurement at a Global Manufacturer

Consider a global manufacturing company that historically managed procurement as a tactical function. Its procurement managers were primarily focused on negotiating the lowest prices for raw materials and managing supplier deliveries. However, as the market became more competitive and supply chain risks increased, the company began to experience several issues:

Quality Issues: Focusing solely on cost resulted in lower quality raw materials, leading to increased product defects and customer complaints.

Supply Disruptions: The company's reliance on a few key suppliers left it vulnerable to disruptions. When one supplier encountered a production problem, it resulted in significant delays and production halts.

Stifled Innovation: The transactional nature of supplier relationships meant that opportunities for joint innovation were missed. Suppliers were hesitant to invest in new technologies or processes without long-term commitments.

Recognizing these challenges, the company re-evaluated its procurement strategy. By shifting from a tactical to a strategic approach, it implemented the following changes:

Enhanced Supplier Collaboration: The company invested in building long-term partnerships with key suppliers. Joint innovation initiatives were launched, leading to the development of new materials and processes that improved product quality and reduced production costs.

Diversification and Risk Management: Rather than relying on a single source, the company diversified its supplier base. This proactive risk management strategy not only improved supply chain resilience but also encouraged competitive pricing.

Adoption of Digital Tools: Implementing an integrated procurement platform allowed the company to automate routine tasks, gain real-time insights, and make data-driven decisions that aligned with its long-term strategic goals.

The transformation resulted in improved product quality, enhanced supplier performance, and a more resilient supply chain. This case exemplifies how moving beyond a tactical approach can drive significant value and competitive advantage.

Conclusion

The traditional role of the procurement manager—focused on sourcing, purchasing, and supplier management—has served organizations well for decades. However, as global markets evolve and the complexity of supply chains increases, the limitations of a tactical approach become ever more apparent. A purely tactical focus, centered on short-term cost savings and transactional efficiency, can lead to quality compromises, reactive management, misalignment with organizational strategy, and underutilization of technological advancements.

To thrive in today's dynamic business environment, procurement managers must embrace a strategic mindset. This involves moving from merely executing transactions to driving value creation through long-term supplier partnerships, proactive risk management, and strategic alignment with business goals. By leveraging technology, enhancing data analytics, and fostering collaborative relationships with suppliers, organizations can transform procurement into a strategic function that not only supports but also propels overall business success.

In this chapter, we have laid the foundation for understanding the role of the procurement manager in its traditional form while critically examining the inherent limitations of a tactical approach. The journey from a transactional mindset to a strategic perspective is not merely a change in processes—it represents a fundamental transformation in how organizations view and leverage procurement. As we move forward in this book, subsequent chapters will build on these foundational concepts, equipping you with the tools, frameworks, and real-world examples necessary to master the art of strategic procurement management.

Embracing this strategic transformation will not only enhance your career as a procurement professional but also enable your organization to navigate the complexities of modern supply chains, capitalize on emerging opportunities, and build a competitive edge in an increasingly challenging global marketplace.

What Is Strategic Procurement?

In today's rapidly evolving business landscape, the role of procurement has shifted from a transactional, cost-focused process to a strategic function that drives long-term organizational success. Strategic procurement is not merely about buying goods or services at the lowest price; it is a comprehensive, proactive approach that aligns purchasing activities with the overall business objectives. This chapter delves into the definition of strategic procurement, outlines its key principles, and explains how it adds value to the organization—ultimately transforming procurement from a cost center into a value generator.

Defining Strategic Procurement

Strategic procurement can be defined as the deliberate and systematic approach to acquiring goods and services that not only meet an organization's immediate needs but also support its long-term goals. Unlike traditional procurement, which focuses primarily on cost reduction and transactional efficiency, strategic procurement encompasses a broader vision. It involves careful analysis of spend data, market research, risk management, supplier relationship development, and the integration of technology—all with the goal of achieving optimal total cost of ownership (TCO) and fostering continuous improvement.

In essence, strategic procurement represents a shift from viewing procurement as a "necessary evil" of transactional buying to recognizing it as a critical driver of overall business strategy and performance.

Key Principles of Strategic Procurement

Strategic procurement is built on several foundational principles that guide its successful implementation. Understanding these principles is crucial for transforming procurement from a tactical, reactive function into a strategic, value-generating partner.

1. Alignment with Business Objectives

A fundamental tenet of strategic procurement is ensuring that procurement activities are closely aligned with the overall business strategy. Every purchasing decision, supplier selection, and contract negotiation should support the organization's core goals, whether they are related to growth, innovation, sustainability, or market competitiveness. According to Pipefy's overview aligning procurement with business objectives ensures that spending decisions contribute directly to enhancing the company's ROI and long-term success.

2. Total Cost of Ownership (TCO) Approach

Traditional procurement often fixates on the initial purchase price. In contrast, strategic procurement adopts a TCO approach, which looks beyond upfront costs to include factors such as maintenance, operational costs, warranty, disposal expenses, and potential risks. This comprehensive evaluation enables organizations to select suppliers and contracts that offer the best overall value over the life cycle of the product or service.

3. Supplier Relationship Management

Effective supplier relationship management (SRM) is a cornerstone of strategic procurement. Rather than treating suppliers as mere vendors, organizations must view them as strategic partners. Building long-term, collaborative relationships with key suppliers leads to greater innovation, improved quality, risk mitigation, and even preferential pricing. As highlighted in the article on strategic procurement principles nurturing these relationships helps both parties adapt to market changes and share valuable insights.

4. Risk Management and Resilience

Strategic procurement requires a proactive approach to risk management. Organizations must continuously monitor market conditions, geopolitical factors, and supply chain vulnerabilities to develop robust contingency plans. By diversifying the supplier base and incorporating risk assessments into procurement strategies, companies can safeguard against disruptions and ensure business continuity even during crises.

5. Continuous Improvement and Innovation

An essential principle of strategic procurement is the commitment to continuous improvement. This involves regularly analyzing procurement performance using key performance indicators (KPIs) and benchmarking against industry standards. Moreover, organizations must be willing to adopt new technologies and innovative practices—such as AI-driven spend analytics and e-procurement platforms—to streamline processes and uncover new value-creation opportunities.

6. Ethical and Sustainable Sourcing

Today's organizations are increasingly held accountable for their environmental and social impact. Strategic procurement integrates ethical considerations and sustainability into its processes by selecting suppliers who adhere to high standards of social responsibility and environmental stewardship. This not only helps protect the organization's reputation but also aligns procurement practices with broader corporate social responsibility (CSR) goals.

7. Data-Driven Decision Making

Leveraging data and analytics is critical in strategic procurement. Modern procurement functions use advanced tools to gather real-time insights on supplier performance, market trends, and spending patterns. By making informed, evidence-based decisions, procurement teams can optimize strategies, reduce costs, and enhance overall operational efficiency. As noted in several industry analyses data-driven decision making is the backbone of strategic sourcing.

How Strategic Procurement Adds Value to the Organization

The true value of strategic procurement lies in its ability to create and sustain long-term benefits for the organization—benefits that extend well beyond simple cost savings. By embedding procurement strategy into the overall business framework, organizations can drive significant improvements in efficiency, innovation, risk management, and supplier performance.

Enhancing Financial Performance

One of the most immediate benefits of strategic procurement is the improvement in financial performance. While traditional procurement might focus on short-term cost reduction, strategic procurement emphasizes a holistic view of spending. Through rigorous spend analysis and negotiation, procurement professionals can secure better pricing, optimize supplier contracts, and reduce the TCO. This often leads to significant cost savings over time, which directly improve the bottom line.

For instance, research from McKinsey has shown that companies with top-quartile procurement capabilities often deliver higher net margins than their peers. This is because strategic procurement not only reduces costs but also minimizes the financial risks associated with supply chain disruptions and market volatility.

Driving Operational Efficiency

Strategic procurement streamlines procurement processes by eliminating redundant tasks and automating routine activities. The integration of advanced procurement technologies—such as e-procurement platforms, AI-based analytics, and digital supplier networks—enables real-time tracking of orders, enhanced visibility into spend data, and faster decision-making. As a result, organizations can reduce lead times, improve inventory management, and ensure timely delivery of goods and services, all of which contribute to enhanced operational efficiency.

Fostering Innovation and Competitive Advantage

By building strong, collaborative relationships with suppliers, strategic procurement encourages innovation. Suppliers are not only expected to provide goods and services but also to collaborate on product development and process improvements. This partnership approach can lead to joint innovation initiatives where suppliers contribute new ideas, technologies, or practices that add value to the organization.

For example, many leading companies have leveraged strategic procurement to co-create products with their suppliers, resulting in improved quality, faster time-to-market, and a unique competitive advantage. Such collaborative innovation ensures that procurement is not just a cost center but a driver of business growth.

Mitigating Supply Chain Risks

Risk management is a critical component of strategic procurement. By diversifying the supplier base, establishing long-term contracts, and continuously monitoring market conditions, procurement professionals can mitigate risks that might otherwise lead to supply chain disruptions. This proactive risk management approach helps ensure that the organization can maintain a steady flow of goods and services, even in the face of economic or geopolitical uncertainties.

Furthermore, strategic procurement often involves scenario planning and contingency strategies that prepare the organization for potential supply chain interruptions. This resilience not only protects the organization from unexpected shocks but also supports overall business stability and growth.

Enhancing Sustainability and Social Value

Modern organizations are increasingly focused on sustainability and social responsibility. Strategic procurement integrates these elements into its framework by prioritizing ethical sourcing, reducing environmental impact, and supporting local communities. By choosing suppliers that adhere to sustainable practices and incorporating sustainability criteria into procurement decisions, organizations can achieve long-term environmental and social benefits.

This focus on sustainability also enhances the organization's brand reputation, appeals to socially conscious consumers, and may even unlock new revenue streams through green initiatives. In today's competitive market, such value creation is often more significant than mere cost reduction.

Leveraging Technology for Continuous Improvement

The adoption of digital tools and data analytics is revolutionizing procurement. These technologies not only automate routine processes but also provide critical insights that drive continuous improvement. Real-time data on supplier performance, market trends, and spend patterns allow procurement teams to quickly identify areas for improvement and adjust strategies accordingly.

For example, many organizations now use integrated procurement platforms to track and analyze key metrics, such as cost savings, supplier lead times, and compliance rates. This data-driven approach ensures that procurement strategies remain agile and responsive to changing business conditions, further enhancing overall organizational performance.

The Shift from Cost-Saving to Value Creation

Historically, procurement has been synonymous with cost-cutting. The traditional view was that the primary objective of procurement was to purchase goods and services at the lowest possible price. While cost reduction remains important, the modern business environment demands a more sophisticated approach—one that balances cost savings with value creation.

Moving Beyond the Price Tag

In a traditional, tactical procurement model, the focus is often on negotiating lower prices and minimizing immediate expenses. However, this narrow approach can lead to unintended consequences, such as compromised quality, supplier dissatisfaction, and ultimately, higher long-term costs. Strategic procurement recognizes that the lowest upfront price does not always equate to the best value. Instead, it considers the full spectrum of costs associated with an acquisition, including quality, reliability, lifecycle costs, and even the potential for innovation.

For example, a supplier offering the lowest price for a critical component might cut corners on quality or lack the capacity to innovate, leading to production delays or higher maintenance costs later on. Strategic procurement evaluates such trade-offs by incorporating TCO analysis into decision making, ensuring that savings today do not translate into higher costs tomorrow.

Emphasizing Supplier Partnerships and Collaboration

One of the most significant shifts in strategic procurement is the transformation of supplier relationships. Instead of being purely transactional, these relationships are evolving into long-term, collaborative partnerships. This approach not only improves the consistency and quality of supplies but also fosters innovation.

Suppliers are incentivized to share ideas and improvements that can lead to mutual gains. When procurement teams engage suppliers as strategic partners, they create an environment where both parties benefit from ongoing collaboration, leading to improved products, more efficient processes, and ultimately, greater value creation.

Integrating Risk Management into Procurement Strategy

Risk management is another area where the shift from cost-saving to value creation is evident. In the past, risk considerations were often an afterthought in procurement decisions. Today, however, strategic procurement integrates risk management into every stage of the process. By proactively identifying and mitigating potential risks—whether related to supply chain disruptions, quality issues, or geopolitical instability—organizations can prevent costly interruptions and maintain business continuity. This integrated approach to risk management is a clear example of how strategic procurement creates value that goes beyond mere cost reduction.

Harnessing Technology and Data Analytics

The digital revolution has provided procurement professionals with powerful tools that transform the procurement process. Modern procurement technology enables real-time data analytics, which can be used to optimize spending, track supplier performance, and predict future market trends. This data-driven approach not only drives efficiency but also unlocks new opportunities for value creation. By leveraging technology, organizations can continuously refine their procurement strategies, ensuring they remain competitive and responsive to changing market conditions.

Advanced analytics tools can identify cost-saving opportunities that were previously hidden in large volumes of spend data. They can also forecast supply chain risks, allowing procurement teams to adjust their strategies in advance. In this way, technology is a key enabler of the shift from a reactive, cost-cutting mentality to a proactive, value-focused approach.

Embracing a Holistic, Long-Term Perspective

Strategic procurement requires a long-term perspective that looks beyond immediate savings. It involves setting goals and metrics that measure success in terms of overall business performance, not just short-term cost reductions. This holistic approach ensures that procurement decisions contribute to the broader strategic objectives of the organization, such as market expansion, product innovation, and sustainable growth.

For instance, investing in suppliers that offer cutting-edge technology or superior quality might result in higher initial costs, but the long-term benefits—such as improved product performance and reduced downtime—can far outweigh these expenses. This long-term view is essential for creating a resilient and agile procurement function that supports the organization's future growth.

Conclusion

Strategic procurement represents a fundamental shift in the way organizations manage their purchasing activities. It is defined by its comprehensive, proactive approach that aligns procurement with the organization's overall business strategy. By embracing key principles such as alignment with business objectives, a TCO approach, strong supplier relationship management, proactive risk management, continuous improvement, ethical and sustainable sourcing, and data-driven decision making, strategic procurement transforms the procurement function from a traditional cost center into a critical driver of organizational value.

This transformation is best understood through the lens of value creation. Rather than focusing solely on cutting costs, strategic procurement seeks to optimize the entire supply chain, enhance operational efficiency, foster innovation, mitigate risks, and support sustainable practices. The shift from cost-saving to value creation is not merely semantic—it fundamentally changes how procurement decisions are made and measured. It moves the focus from short-term savings to long-term benefits, ensuring that every procurement decision contributes to the company's strategic goals and overall competitiveness.

In today's dynamic and interconnected business environment, organizations that invest in strategic procurement are better positioned to navigate uncertainties, respond to market changes, and achieve sustainable growth. By integrating technology, building collaborative supplier partnerships, and taking a holistic, long-term approach to procurement, companies can unlock significant value that goes far beyond traditional cost savings.

Ultimately, strategic procurement is about turning procurement into a strategic asset—a lever that drives innovation, improves performance, and creates competitive advantage. Embracing this modern approach is essential for any organization looking to thrive in a complex, global marketplace.

The Strategic Procurement Manager's Mindset

In today's rapidly evolving business environment, the role of procurement is no longer confined to handling routine transactions or simply cutting costs. Instead, the modern procurement manager must adopt a strategic mindset that transforms the procurement function into a critical engine of value creation for the organization. This transformation requires a fundamental shift in thinking—one that emphasizes long-term planning, innovation, collaboration, and the ability to function as an integrated business partner rather than a mere support function.

In this chapter, we will explore three core aspects of the strategic procurement manager's mindset:

Thinking Beyond Transactions

Embracing Innovation, Collaboration, and Long-Term Planning

Becoming a Business Partner Rather Than a Support Function

Each of these pillars is essential to unlocking the full potential of procurement and elevating its impact on the overall success of the organization.

Thinking Beyond Transactions

For many years, procurement was seen as a back-office function, primarily focused on managing orders, negotiating prices, and ensuring timely delivery. This traditional transactional view limited procurement to a series of routine tasks that were measured solely by short-term cost savings. However, the modern business landscape demands that procurement professionals move well beyond these narrow confines.

From Order-Taker to Strategic Thinker

The first step in evolving the procurement mindset is to shift from an order-taker mentality to that of a strategic thinker. Instead of simply executing purchase orders, the procurement manager must analyze market trends, forecast demand, and assess long-term supplier capabilities. By doing so, they can identify opportunities for innovation, optimize supply chain efficiency, and even influence product development.

This transition involves moving away from a reactive approach—where decisions are made only when a need arises—and instead adopting a proactive strategy that anticipates future requirements. For instance, rather than waiting for a stock-out situation, a strategic procurement manager conducts regular reviews of inventory levels, supplier performance, and market dynamics to predict and mitigate potential disruptions before they occur.

Leveraging Data and Analytics

In the digital age, information is power. The modern procurement manager harnesses advanced data analytics tools and business intelligence systems to gain real-time insights into spending patterns, supplier performance, and market conditions. This data-driven approach allows procurement teams to make informed decisions that go well beyond the mere price tag on a product.

For example, by analyzing historical spend data and forecasting trends, a procurement manager can negotiate long-term contracts that not only secure competitive prices but also ensure supplier stability and quality over time. Additionally, these insights enable the identification of cost drivers and inefficiencies within the supply chain, setting the stage for continuous process improvements that can lead to significant cost reductions and enhanced service levels.

The Importance of Total Cost of Ownership

Thinking beyond transactions also means embracing a total cost of ownership (TCO) perspective. Rather than focusing solely on the upfront purchase price, the strategic procurement manager evaluates all costs associated with the acquisition, including maintenance, training, support, and disposal expenses. This holistic view ensures that procurement decisions contribute to the overall value creation of the organization, rather than simply achieving momentary savings that might lead to higher costs in the long run.

Embracing Innovation, Collaboration, and Long-Term Planning

The contemporary procurement landscape is characterized by rapid technological advancements, global market fluctuations, and ever-increasing competition. In such an environment, innovation, collaboration, and long-term planning are not just desirable—they are essential.

Embracing Innovation

Innovation in procurement means challenging the status quo and seeking creative solutions to long-standing problems. The strategic procurement manager must foster an environment where new ideas are welcomed and tested. This could involve integrating new digital tools, such as artificial intelligence (AI) for predictive analytics, blockchain for enhanced transparency, or robotic process automation (RPA) to streamline repetitive tasks.

For instance, using AI-driven analytics can help forecast demand more accurately, thereby reducing waste and optimizing inventory management. Meanwhile, blockchain technology can provide a secure and transparent record of transactions, which enhances trust between the organization and its suppliers. These technological advancements are not just add-ons; they are catalysts that transform procurement into a forward-thinking, agile function.

Innovation also extends to supplier engagement. By inviting suppliers to participate in joint innovation initiatives, procurement managers can tap into a wealth of external expertise. This collaborative approach often leads to the co-development of products, processes, or even new business models that create value for both parties. Suppliers are no longer viewed as passive vendors but as active partners in the innovation process.

Fostering Collaboration

Collaboration is at the heart of strategic procurement. The procurement manager must work closely with various internal stakeholders—such as finance, operations, R&D, and marketing—to ensure that procurement decisions are aligned with broader business objectives. This cross-functional collaboration ensures that the procurement strategy supports the company's long-term goals, whether they involve cost reduction, product innovation, or market expansion.

Internally, collaborative efforts help break down silos. When procurement works hand-in-hand with other departments, it gains a deeper understanding of organizational needs and challenges. This shared understanding leads to more effective and coherent strategies that enhance overall efficiency and performance.

Externally, collaboration with suppliers is equally important. Establishing long-term partnerships requires open communication, mutual trust, and a shared vision. Strategic procurement managers invest time in developing strong supplier relationships that go beyond annual contract negotiations. These partnerships are built on joint planning sessions, regular performance reviews, and even co-investment in new technologies or processes.

A collaborative approach can also extend to strategic alliances and networks. By participating in industry forums, consortiums, or public–private partnerships, procurement managers can access a broader pool of expertise and resources. These alliances often result in better bargaining power, enhanced market insights, and the ability to drive industry-wide innovations that benefit all stakeholders.

Prioritizing Long-Term Planning

Long-term planning is the cornerstone of strategic procurement. It requires a shift in focus from immediate, short-term needs to anticipating future challenges and opportunities. A strategic procurement manager is always looking ahead—forecasting market trends, evaluating emerging risks, and preparing for potential disruptions.

This long-term perspective is crucial for several reasons. First, it ensures that procurement strategies are resilient in the face of economic volatility and market uncertainties. By planning ahead, organizations can secure contracts that guarantee supply continuity and mitigate risks associated with sudden market changes or geopolitical events.

Second, long-term planning enables the optimization of supplier relationships. Rather than renegotiating contracts annually, strategic procurement managers aim to establish multi-year agreements that provide stability and foster a deeper level of collaboration. These long-term contracts often come with built-in mechanisms for continuous improvement, performance reviews, and even joint innovation initiatives.

Third, a forward-looking approach allows procurement managers to align their strategies with the organization's growth plans. For example, if a company is planning to expand into new markets or launch innovative products, the procurement strategy must be tailored to support these initiatives. This might involve identifying new suppliers with specialized capabilities, investing in new technologies, or even reconfiguring the supply chain to accommodate increased demand.

Long-term planning also involves setting clear performance metrics and regularly reviewing progress against these goals. By establishing key performance indicators (KPIs) that measure not just cost savings but also quality improvements, innovation outcomes, and risk mitigation, procurement managers can ensure that their strategies are delivering tangible value over time.

Becoming a Business Partner Rather Than a Support Function

One of the most significant shifts in the modern procurement landscape is the evolution from being a support function to becoming a strategic business partner. This transformation involves rebranding the procurement department as a critical component of the organization's overall strategy, with a direct influence on business outcomes.

Building a Seat at the Decision-Making Table

For procurement managers to be seen as true business partners, they must secure a seat at the executive table. This means actively participating in strategic discussions, contributing to long-term planning, and providing insights that shape overall business strategy. When procurement is involved in key decision-making processes—such as product development, market expansion, or innovation initiatives—it is positioned as an integral part of the organization's success.

A strategic procurement manager communicates in the language of business, using data and insights to support recommendations. This involves translating procurement metrics into business outcomes, such as improved cash flow, reduced risks, or enhanced customer satisfaction. By aligning procurement goals with those of the broader organization, the procurement manager demonstrates how effective sourcing and supplier management can drive competitive advantage.

Influencing Through Data and Insights

Modern procurement departments generate vast amounts of data—from spend analytics to supplier performance metrics. A strategic procurement manager leverages this data to provide actionable insights to senior leadership. For example, by analyzing trends in supplier performance or identifying inefficiencies in the supply chain, procurement can highlight opportunities for cost savings, innovation, or risk reduction.

This ability to harness data and translate it into strategic insights is a key differentiator. It moves procurement from a reactive function that simply responds to immediate needs to a proactive force that anticipates challenges and drives business improvement. When procurement managers share these insights with other business leaders, they not only justify the value of procurement but also drive cross-functional initiatives that enhance overall performance.

Fostering a Culture of Collaboration and Innovation

Becoming a business partner means that the procurement function is not isolated from the rest of the organization. Instead, it is deeply embedded within every facet of the business. To achieve this integration, procurement managers must foster a culture of collaboration both internally and externally.

Internally, this involves breaking down silos between procurement and other departments. Regular cross-functional meetings, joint strategy sessions, and collaborative projects help build trust and ensure that procurement activities are aligned with the company's strategic goals. This collaborative culture encourages other departments to view procurement as a partner in innovation and value creation rather than a gatekeeper of costs.

Externally, fostering strong relationships with suppliers is paramount. Strategic procurement managers work to build long-term partnerships based on mutual trust, open communication, and shared objectives. These partnerships enable the co-creation of value, where both the supplier and the organization collaborate on new product development, process improvements, and joint innovation initiatives.

Shifting the Value Proposition

The value proposition of procurement must evolve from simply reducing costs to driving overall business value. This shift requires procurement managers to reframe how success is measured. Rather than focusing solely on cost savings, they should also emphasize improvements in quality, innovation outcomes, risk mitigation, and customer satisfaction.

For example, a procurement initiative that results in a modest cost reduction might also enhance supplier quality or reduce lead times. These improvements can lead to better product performance, higher customer satisfaction, and ultimately, a stronger competitive position in the market. By taking a broader view of value, procurement can demonstrate its strategic impact on the organization.

Communicating Value Internally and Externally

A critical aspect of becoming a business partner is effective communication. Strategic procurement managers must articulate the value of their initiatives in terms that resonate with senior leadership and other stakeholders. This means moving beyond technical jargon and focusing on how procurement activities contribute to the organization's broader goals.

One effective approach is to develop a procurement scorecard that includes not only cost metrics but also indicators of supplier innovation, risk management, and process efficiency. By presenting a balanced view of performance, procurement managers can build credibility and reinforce the idea that procurement is a strategic function that drives long-term success.

Externally, communicating with suppliers in a transparent and collaborative manner helps build stronger partnerships. Regular performance reviews, joint planning sessions, and open dialogue about challenges and opportunities are essential to maintaining trust and fostering continuous improvement.

The Road Ahead: Cultivating the Strategic Mindset

The transition from a traditional, transactional approach to a strategic, partnership-based mindset is not instantaneous. It requires a concerted effort to reframe the role of procurement within the organization. For procurement managers willing to invest in their personal and professional growth, the rewards can be substantial.

Investing in Professional Development

To successfully cultivate a strategic mindset, procurement managers must continuously develop their skills. This includes not only technical skills related to data analytics, contract negotiation, and risk management but also soft skills such as leadership, communication, and strategic thinking. Professional development programs, industry certifications, and cross-functional training can help procurement leaders stay ahead of industry trends and best practices.

Furthermore, networking with peers, attending industry conferences, and participating in procurement forums provide opportunities to share insights and learn from others who have successfully transitioned to a strategic role. This continuous learning process is vital for maintaining a competitive edge and ensuring that procurement remains a dynamic and evolving function.

Embracing Change and Driving Transformation

The journey toward becoming a strategic business partner is an ongoing process. It involves embracing change and continually seeking ways to improve procurement practices. Strategic procurement managers must be willing to challenge traditional methods, experiment with new technologies, and adopt innovative approaches to problem-solving.

Change management is a critical component of this transformation. Procurement leaders must not only implement new processes and systems but also drive cultural change within the organization. This means engaging with all levels of the company to foster a shared vision of procurement as a strategic asset. By championing change and demonstrating the tangible benefits of a strategic approach, procurement managers can inspire others to embrace the transformation.

Measuring Success in a Strategic Framework

Finally, the success of the strategic procurement mindset must be measured using a comprehensive framework that goes beyond cost savings. Key performance indicators (KPIs) should encompass a range of metrics that reflect the full value delivered by procurement. These may include:

> **Cost Savings and Avoidance:** While still important, these metrics should be considered alongside others.

> **Quality Improvements:** Measures of product quality, defect rates, and supplier performance.

> **Innovation Contributions:** Metrics that track collaborative innovation initiatives, new product development, or process improvements driven by supplier partnerships.

Risk Mitigation: Indicators of supply chain resilience, such as reduced lead times, diversified supplier bases, or improved contingency planning.

Customer and Stakeholder Satisfaction: Surveys and feedback mechanisms that assess the satisfaction of internal stakeholders and end customers with procurement outcomes.

By adopting a balanced scorecard approach, procurement managers can demonstrate how strategic procurement contributes to the overall success of the organization. This comprehensive measurement system reinforces the idea that procurement is not merely a support function but a critical driver of value creation.

Conclusion

The strategic procurement manager's mindset is a fundamental shift in how procurement is viewed and executed. It is about transforming a traditional, transactional function into a dynamic, value-creating partner that drives innovation, enhances operational efficiency, and contributes directly to the organization's strategic objectives. This evolution requires a proactive approach—thinking beyond immediate transactions, embracing innovative technologies and collaborative relationships, and committing to long-term planning.

By adopting a holistic perspective that emphasizes total cost of ownership, risk management, continuous improvement, and sustainability, procurement managers can unlock significant value for their organizations. They must evolve from merely executing purchase orders to becoming trusted advisors who influence strategic decisions at the highest levels of the business.

Moreover, this transformation is not solely about processes or technologies—it is about culture. Cultivating a strategic mindset requires continuous learning, effective communication, and a willingness to challenge conventional practices. When procurement managers invest in their own development and actively foster collaboration both internally and externally, they pave the way for procurement to become a true business partner.

In today's competitive and fast-paced market, organizations that leverage strategic procurement are better positioned to navigate uncertainties, respond to market changes, and achieve sustainable growth. The procurement function, once relegated to the role of a cost-cutting back-office, is now emerging as a central player in driving business success.

Ultimately, the strategic procurement manager's mindset is not just a set of skills or practices—it is a philosophy. It represents a commitment to looking beyond short-term gains and focusing on the long-term impact of every procurement decision. By reimagining procurement as a strategic partner, organizations can harness the full potential of their supply chains, foster innovation, and secure a competitive edge in the global marketplace.

Embrace the journey from tactical to strategic procurement, and in doing so, transform not only the procurement function but also the entire organization. The future belongs to those who see procurement not as a mere support function but as an indispensable driver of business growth and innovation.

Part 2: Building the Skillset

Core Competencies of a Strategic Procurement Manager

The transformation from a transactional to a strategic procurement function does not happen by chance. It is the product of continuous learning and the deliberate cultivation of a skill set that goes beyond simply processing orders. For a procurement professional to evolve into a strategic procurement manager, they must master a suite of core competencies that empower them to drive long-term value for their organization. In this chapter, we explore four foundational competencies: analytical thinking and data-driven decision-making; negotiation and relationship management; risk management and mitigation; and financial acumen, including an in-depth understanding of total cost of ownership (TCO).

Analytical Thinking and Data-Driven Decision-Making

In today's competitive and data-saturated business environment, analytical thinking has become indispensable. Strategic procurement managers must not only gather data but also interpret it to guide decision-making. This competency goes far beyond simple spreadsheet analysis; it involves leveraging advanced analytics tools, predictive models, and visualization dashboards to forecast trends, assess supplier performance, and identify cost-saving opportunities.

The Role of Data in Procurement

Data-driven decision-making transforms procurement from a reactive function into a proactive one. By analyzing historical spend, market dynamics, and supplier performance metrics, procurement managers can identify patterns that inform strategic decisions. For example, through data analytics, managers can pinpoint which suppliers consistently deliver quality materials on time and at competitive prices. These insights lead to stronger negotiations and long-term partnerships that are critical for sustaining competitive advantage.

Organizations like Sievo have demonstrated how AI-powered procurement analytics can cut down sourcing time by 90% and provide real-time insights into spend data Such tools empower procurement professionals to move beyond intuition and base their decisions on robust, empirical evidence.

Developing Analytical Skills

To enhance their analytical prowess, procurement managers should:

Invest in Training: Continuous learning through courses in data analytics, statistics, and advanced Excel techniques is key. Many professionals pursue certifications in procurement analytics to stay current with emerging technologies.

Utilize Advanced Tools: Familiarity with Business Intelligence (BI) platforms, ERP systems, and specialized procurement analytics software is crucial. These tools not only automate data collection but also help transform raw data into actionable insights.

Practice Critical Thinking: Beyond numbers, managers must interpret what the data signifies in terms of supply chain performance, cost drivers, and risk indicators. This critical analysis often leads to better negotiation strategies and proactive risk management.

Ultimately, analytical thinking and data-driven decision-making enable procurement managers to predict future market conditions, optimize supplier selections, and drive long-term savings that go beyond traditional cost-cutting measures.

Negotiation and Relationship Management

Another cornerstone competency for a strategic procurement manager is the ability to negotiate effectively and manage relationships. In a role where suppliers are key partners rather than mere vendors, strong negotiation skills and the art of relationship management become critical.

The Art of Negotiation

Negotiation is much more than haggling over price. It is a strategic exercise that involves understanding market conditions, supplier motivations, and internal organizational needs. Effective negotiation helps secure favorable contract terms, reduce costs, and enhance the overall value of procurement deals.

Key strategies for successful negotiation include:

> **Preparation:** Gather as much information as possible on the supplier, market rates, and historical spend. Data-driven insights gathered from analytical tools support this process.

> **Clear Objectives:** Define what success looks like before entering negotiations. This includes understanding the company's cost targets, quality standards, and service level requirements.

> **Win-Win Approach:** Focus on creating mutually beneficial outcomes that strengthen long-term relationships. A strategic procurement manager sees every negotiation as an opportunity to build a partnership rather than a one-time transaction.

> **Flexibility:** Be prepared to adapt negotiation tactics based on the conversation dynamics. This could involve offering longer contract durations in exchange for better pricing or additional services.

Building and Managing Relationships

In addition to negotiation, relationship management is a critical skill for sustaining long-term supplier partnerships. Strong supplier relationships lead to better collaboration, innovation, and risk-sharing—all of which are essential for a resilient supply chain.

To cultivate these relationships, procurement managers should:

Engage Regularly: Regular communication with suppliers fosters trust and keeps both parties aligned. This may include periodic performance reviews, joint planning sessions, and collaborative problem-solving.

Invest in Collaboration: View suppliers as strategic partners. Engage them in innovation initiatives and product development discussions. This collaborative approach can result in improved product quality and new cost-saving opportunities.

Monitor Performance: Use performance metrics and supplier scorecards to track supplier performance over time. This data-driven feedback allows for continuous improvement in supplier relationships.

Resolve Conflicts Constructively: When disagreements arise, a strategic procurement manager uses conflict resolution skills to address issues promptly and fairly, ensuring that the relationship remains strong.

Ultimately, negotiation and relationship management are about creating a stable, dynamic network of suppliers that can support the organization's strategic goals. The ability to negotiate effectively while building strong, lasting relationships is a hallmark of a procurement leader who transforms the function from a cost center into a strategic asset.

Risk Management and Mitigation

The procurement function is fraught with risks—from supplier failures and geopolitical instability to price fluctuations and quality issues. A strategic procurement manager must be adept at identifying, assessing, and mitigating these risks to safeguard the organization's supply chain.

Identifying Risks

Risk management begins with a thorough understanding of potential risks. These may include:

Supply Chain Disruptions: Natural disasters, political instability, or supplier insolvency can interrupt the supply chain.

Market Risks: Price volatility, currency fluctuations, and changing market demand can impact procurement costs.

Operational Risks: Inadequate process controls, non-compliance with regulations, and logistical challenges.

Reputational Risks: Working with suppliers who do not adhere to ethical or sustainability standards can harm the company's reputation.

Mitigation Strategies

A proactive risk management strategy involves several key steps:

Diversification: Avoid relying on a single supplier by diversifying the supplier base. This reduces dependency and spreads risk across multiple sources.

Contingency Planning: Develop contingency plans for potential disruptions. This might include maintaining safety stock, having backup suppliers, or establishing flexible contracts that allow for adjustments in supply.

Regular Monitoring: Use real-time data analytics to monitor risk indicators continuously. Key metrics such as supplier performance, delivery times, and quality metrics help detect early signs of trouble.

Collaboration with Suppliers: Engage suppliers in risk management discussions. By working together, both parties can develop strategies to mitigate risks that affect the entire supply chain.

Scenario Analysis: Conduct "what-if" analyses to understand the potential impact of different risk scenarios. This helps in prioritizing risks and implementing the most effective mitigation measures.

Implementing Risk Management Processes

Effective risk management is an ongoing process. Procurement managers must integrate risk assessment into every stage of the procurement lifecycle—from the initial supplier selection and contract negotiation to performance monitoring and relationship management.

Some best practices include:

Risk Registers: Maintain a detailed risk register that tracks identified risks, their potential impact, likelihood, and the measures in place to mitigate them.

Regular Reviews: Schedule periodic risk reviews to update the risk register and adjust strategies based on changing market conditions or supplier performance.

Training and Awareness: Ensure that procurement teams are well-trained in risk management techniques and understand the importance of proactive risk mitigation.

Leveraging Technology: Use procurement and risk management software to automate risk monitoring and generate alerts when risk thresholds are exceeded.

A strategic procurement manager who prioritizes risk management ensures that the organization can navigate uncertainties, maintain continuity, and capitalize on opportunities even in turbulent times.

Financial Acumen and Understanding Total Cost of Ownership (TCO)

Financial acumen is another cornerstone of the strategic procurement skillset. It involves a deep understanding of financial principles, budgeting, cost management, and, crucially, the concept of Total Cost of Ownership (TCO).

Beyond the Price Tag: Understanding TCO

Total Cost of Ownership is the comprehensive assessment of all costs associated with a purchase over its entire lifecycle. This includes not only the purchase price but also:

Operating Costs: Expenses related to maintenance, support, and operation.

Financing Costs: Interest and fees associated with the procurement.

Logistics and Storage: Costs for transportation, warehousing, and handling.

Disposal Costs: Expenses involved in decommissioning or disposing of the asset at the end of its life.

Indirect Costs: Hidden costs such as downtime, quality issues, and inefficiencies that may arise from poor procurement decisions.

By focusing on TCO, a strategic procurement manager ensures that the organization does not make decisions based solely on the lowest upfront cost. Instead, the long-term financial impact is considered, leading to more sustainable and cost-effective procurement practices.

Developing Financial Acumen

To build strong financial acumen, procurement managers should:

Understand Financial Statements: Gain a solid grasp of balance sheets, income statements, and cash flow statements. This knowledge is crucial for assessing how procurement decisions affect the overall financial health of the organization.

Budgeting and Forecasting: Develop skills in budgeting, forecasting, and cost analysis. This includes understanding how to allocate resources efficiently and measure cost savings against targets.

Engage in Financial Analysis: Use tools like cost-benefit analysis, return on investment (ROI), and TCO calculations to evaluate procurement options. Financial modeling and scenario analysis can help forecast long-term outcomes.

Collaborate with Finance: Work closely with the finance department to align procurement strategies with financial goals. This collaboration ensures that procurement initiatives contribute positively to the organization's profitability.

Stay Updated on Market Trends: Monitor changes in the market that may impact costs, such as commodity price fluctuations, currency exchange rates, and economic indicators.

These insights can inform negotiation strategies and supplier selection.

Applying Financial Acumen in Procurement

A procurement manager with strong financial acumen can drive significant value through:

Negotiation Leverage: Using financial data and TCO analysis during negotiations to secure contracts that not only reduce costs but also minimize long-term expenses.

Budget Optimization: Aligning procurement budgets with strategic initiatives and ensuring that every dollar spent contributes to value creation.

Investment in Technology: Justifying investments in procurement technology and analytics tools by demonstrating the long-term savings and efficiency gains through financial analysis.

Measuring Savings: Accurately tracking and reporting cost savings and cost avoidance, which are critical metrics in proving the value of procurement activities to senior management.

By developing and applying financial acumen, procurement managers transform procurement decisions from a series of cost-cutting exercises into strategic investments that enhance the overall financial performance of the organization.

Bringing It All Together

The core competencies of a strategic procurement manager—analytical thinking, negotiation and relationship management, risk management, and financial acumen—are interdependent and collectively drive the transformation from a tactical to a strategic function. Each competency reinforces the others:

Data-Driven Decision-Making: Analytical skills support better negotiation outcomes by providing the facts and figures needed to argue for favorable terms.

Negotiation and Relationships: Effective relationship management not only secures better deals but also creates a foundation for collaborative risk management and innovation.

Risk Management: Proactive risk assessment ensures that financial decisions and procurement strategies are resilient and sustainable over the long term.

Financial Acumen and TCO: A deep understanding of financial principles and TCO ensures that every procurement decision contributes to the company's overall profitability and value creation.

The Holistic Approach

To excel as a strategic procurement manager, one must adopt a holistic approach that integrates these core competencies into daily practice. This means continuously seeking improvement, staying informed about market and technological changes, and investing in professional development. It also involves a mindset shift—from seeing procurement as a series of isolated transactions to viewing it as a central, strategic function that drives business success.

Strategies for Continuous Skill Development

Becoming a master of strategic procurement is an ongoing journey. Here are some strategies for continuous development:

Professional Certifications and Training:
Enroll in courses and certifications such as CPSM, CSCP, or CIPS. These programs not only enhance your knowledge but also signal your commitment to excellence in procurement.

On-the-Job Learning:
Seek opportunities to work on cross-functional projects, lead negotiations, and participate in strategic sourcing initiatives. Real-world experience is invaluable in honing your competencies.

Mentorship and Networking:
Build relationships with experienced procurement leaders. Mentorship can provide insights into industry best practices and help navigate complex challenges.

Technology Adoption:
Stay abreast of the latest procurement tools and technologies. Experiment with data analytics platforms, e-sourcing tools, and AI-driven applications to integrate technology into your procurement strategy effectively.

Risk Management Drills:
Regularly conduct risk assessment workshops and scenario planning exercises with your team. This practice will keep you prepared for unforeseen disruptions and reinforce your proactive risk management skills.

Financial Workshops:
Participate in financial analysis workshops and collaborate closely with your finance team. Understanding advanced financial concepts and their practical applications in procurement will strengthen your overall acumen.

Soft Skills Enhancement:
Communication, negotiation, and relationship-building skills are as important as technical skills. Engage in training sessions, role-playing exercises, and public speaking courses to improve these areas.

Measuring Your Progress

A strategic procurement manager must also be able to measure the effectiveness of their skill development. Key performance indicators (KPIs) can include:

Cost Savings Achieved: Quantify savings realized from strategic negotiations and TCO optimization.

Supplier Performance Scores: Track improvements in supplier quality, reliability, and innovation.

Risk Mitigation Effectiveness: Monitor the reduction in supply chain disruptions and improved responsiveness.

Analytical Efficiency: Assess how data-driven insights have improved decision-making processes.

Financial Impact: Measure the contribution of procurement initiatives to the overall profitability of the organization.

Regular self-assessment and feedback from peers and mentors can help you understand where you excel and identify areas for further improvement.

Conclusion

The journey from tactical to strategic procurement management is underpinned by a robust set of competencies that empower procurement managers to drive long-term value for their organizations. Analytical thinking and data-driven decision-making provide the foundation for making informed, proactive choices; negotiation and relationship management transform suppliers into strategic partners; risk management and mitigation ensure the resilience of the supply chain; and financial acumen—especially an in-depth understanding of TCO—ensures that every procurement decision contributes positively to the organization's bottom line.

By building and continuously refining these core competencies, procurement managers not only enhance their own professional value but also play a critical role in shaping the future of their organizations. Embracing a holistic, integrated approach to skill development transforms procurement from a mere support function into a dynamic, strategic driver of business success.

Invest in your skill set, foster a culture of continuous improvement, and leverage technology and data to navigate an increasingly complex market. The strategic procurement manager's ability to combine analytical rigor, negotiation finesse, risk intelligence, and financial insight is the key to unlocking sustainable competitive advantage in today's ever-evolving business landscape.

As you work to build these skills, remember that every decision you make, every negotiation you lead, and every risk you mitigate is a step toward transforming procurement into a true strategic asset. The future belongs to those who not only understand the numbers but also the relationships and strategies behind them. Embrace this journey, and let your skills drive the success of your organization.

Mastering Procurement Technology

In today's rapidly evolving business landscape, technology has become the linchpin of strategic procurement. No longer is procurement about manually processing orders or relying solely on intuition; it is now a dynamic, data-driven function that leverages advanced software and digital tools to optimize every facet of the supply chain. Mastering procurement technology is not merely about adopting new tools—it's about integrating them into a comprehensive strategy that drives long-term value. This chapter explores how to leverage procurement software and tools, such as ERP systems, e_procurement platforms, and spend analytics, while also highlighting the transformative impact of artificial intelligence (AI), machine learning (ML), and automation on procurement processes.

The Digital Transformation of Procurement

The transition from tactical to strategic procurement has been significantly accelerated by digital transformation. Today's procurement managers have a wide range of technology tools at their disposal that streamline operations, reduce costs, and enable more informed decision-making.

The Role of ERP Systems

Enterprise Resource Planning (ERP) systems are at the heart of many procurement operations. These integrated platforms consolidate data from various business functions—including finance, manufacturing, and supply chain management—into one unified system. By centralizing information, ERP systems facilitate seamless communication between departments, providing procurement managers with real-time visibility into spend, inventory, and supplier performance.

For instance, ERP systems help in:

Automating Routine Tasks: Automating order placement, invoicing, and payment processing reduces manual errors and frees up valuable time for strategic activities.

Data Consolidation: Consolidated data enables better forecasting and budgeting by providing a single source of truth for all procurement-related information.

Enhanced Reporting: Advanced reporting tools built into ERP systems allow procurement managers to generate detailed analyses on spend, supplier performance, and cost trends, supporting more strategic decision-making.

The comprehensive view provided by ERP systems is essential for optimizing the total cost of ownership (TCO) and ensuring that procurement strategies align with broader business objectives.

E-Procurement Platforms

E-procurement platforms represent another significant leap forward in procurement technology. These platforms facilitate the entire procurement process online, from requisition to contract management. They help streamline workflows, enhance transparency, and enable greater collaboration both within the organization and with external suppliers.

Key benefits of e_procurement platforms include:

Streamlined Processes: By automating approval workflows and order processing, e_procurement systems reduce cycle times and improve efficiency.

Increased Transparency: Digital systems provide a clear audit trail of all transactions, making it easier to track performance and ensure compliance.

Enhanced Supplier Collaboration: These platforms allow for real-time communication and collaboration with suppliers, enabling better negotiation and faster resolution of issues.

Cost Savings: Reduced administrative overhead and improved process efficiency often translate into significant cost savings.

E_procurement tools empower organizations to move away from cumbersome manual processes and adopt a more agile, responsive procurement strategy that can adapt quickly to changing market conditions.

Spend Analytics: Driving Data-Driven Decisions

Spend analytics is a critical component of modern procurement technology. It involves the collection, cleansing, and analysis of spend data to uncover trends, identify cost-saving opportunities, and assess supplier performance. With the vast amount of data generated by procurement activities, sophisticated analytics tools help transform raw data into actionable insights.

Procurement managers leverage spend analytics to:

Identify Savings Opportunities: Detailed analysis of historical spend can reveal patterns and inefficiencies that, when addressed, lead to substantial cost savings.

Monitor Supplier Performance: Continuous tracking of supplier performance metrics, such as delivery times and quality scores, helps in maintaining high standards and ensuring reliability.

Optimize Supplier Portfolios: Spend analytics enable the segmentation of suppliers based on performance, risk, and cost, thereby supporting more strategic supplier relationship management.

Support Strategic Sourcing: Data-driven insights inform sourcing decisions, ensuring that procurement strategies are based on solid market intelligence rather than assumptions.

The use of advanced analytics platforms, often integrated with ERP and e_procurement systems, is transforming procurement into a highly strategic, data-driven function. By harnessing these tools, procurement managers can make more informed decisions that contribute directly to the organization's bottom line.

The Role of AI, Machine Learning, and Automation

While traditional procurement technologies like ERP systems and e_procurement platforms have significantly enhanced efficiency, the next wave of innovation is driven by artificial intelligence, machine learning, and automation. These technologies are not only transforming how procurement functions but are also enabling procurement teams to become true strategic partners within their organizations.

Artificial Intelligence in Procurement

Artificial intelligence (AI) is revolutionizing procurement by enabling systems to analyze vast amounts of data quickly and accurately. AI-driven procurement tools can forecast demand, predict supplier performance, and identify potential risks even before they become apparent.

Key applications of AI in procurement include:

Predictive Analytics: AI algorithms analyze historical data and current trends to forecast future procurement needs and potential market shifts. This allows for proactive decision-making and better risk management.

Automated Supplier Selection: AI tools can sift through extensive supplier data to identify the best candidates based on criteria such as cost, quality, and reliability. This not only speeds up the selection process but also improves the accuracy of supplier evaluations.

Enhanced Decision-Making: By providing real-time insights and recommendations, AI supports more strategic decision-making. For example, AI can suggest optimal order quantities or identify the best times to negotiate contracts based on market dynamics.

Fraud Detection and Compliance: AI systems can monitor transactions in real time, flagging anomalies and potential compliance issues. This helps mitigate risks associated with fraudulent activities or regulatory breaches.

As AI continues to evolve, its integration into procurement processes will further enhance efficiency, reduce costs, and enable a more agile response to market changes.

Machine Learning: Continuous Improvement Through Data

Machine learning (ML), a subset of AI, is instrumental in enabling systems to learn from data and improve over time without explicit programming. In procurement, ML models can identify patterns and trends that humans might miss, leading to more accurate predictions and better procurement strategies.

Some examples of how machine learning is applied in procurement include:

Dynamic Pricing Models: ML algorithms can analyze market data to determine optimal pricing strategies, adjusting to fluctuations in demand and supply in real time.

Supplier Performance Evaluation: Machine learning models continuously assess supplier data, providing dynamic performance ratings that help procurement managers make informed decisions about supplier relationships.

Anomaly Detection: ML techniques can detect anomalies in procurement data, such as unexpected cost increases or delivery delays, allowing for quick intervention before minor issues escalate into major problems.

Process Optimization: By analyzing historical procurement processes, ML can identify inefficiencies and suggest process improvements that reduce cycle times and lower costs.

Machine learning, therefore, is not just about automating tasks but about continuously enhancing procurement strategies by learning from every transaction and decision.

Automation: Streamlining Routine Tasks

Automation is perhaps the most visible change in modern procurement. By automating routine tasks, procurement teams can redirect their focus from administrative work to strategic decision-making and value creation.

Benefits of automation in procurement include:

Reduced Manual Errors: Automation minimizes the risk of human error in repetitive tasks such as data entry, order processing, and invoice matching.

Faster Processing Times: Automated systems can process transactions and generate reports much faster than manual methods, leading to quicker decision-making.

Improved Compliance: Automation ensures that procurement processes adhere to established policies and regulatory requirements, reducing the risk of non-compliance.

Cost Efficiency: By reducing labor-intensive tasks, automation lowers operational costs and frees up resources for more strategic activities.

Enhanced Visibility: Automated systems provide real-time tracking of procurement activities, offering comprehensive visibility into spend, supplier performance, and inventory levels.

E_procurement platforms and ERP systems are increasingly incorporating automation features. These include automated approval workflows, digital invoicing, and even AI-powered chatbots that can handle routine supplier queries. As a result, procurement teams are not only more efficient but are also better equipped to focus on strategic initiatives that drive long-term value.

Integrating Technology for a Strategic Advantage

For procurement managers aiming to transition from a tactical to a strategic role, mastering procurement technology is critical. It requires not only the adoption of advanced software tools but also a mindset that embraces innovation and continuous improvement.

Aligning Technology with Business Objectives

The most effective procurement technologies are those that align with the organization's strategic goals. This means choosing tools that support not just the administrative aspects of procurement but also enable deeper strategic insights. For example, an ERP system integrated with advanced analytics can provide a holistic view of the supply chain, highlighting areas for cost reduction, risk mitigation, and supplier optimization.

Similarly, e_procurement platforms that incorporate AI and ML capabilities allow procurement managers to execute more strategic sourcing initiatives. When these systems are fully integrated, they enable a seamless flow of information from procurement to finance, operations, and even product development, ensuring that every procurement decision is informed by comprehensive, real-time data.

The Future of Procurement Technology

Looking ahead, the role of technology in procurement will continue to expand. Emerging technologies such as blockchain, the Internet of Things (IoT), and advanced robotics are set to further revolutionize procurement processes.

Blockchain: This technology offers enhanced transparency and security in procurement transactions. Blockchain can provide an immutable record of transactions, which is particularly useful for verifying the authenticity of supplier certifications, tracking the origin of goods, and ensuring compliance with regulatory requirements.

IoT: The Internet of Things connects devices and systems, providing real-time data on inventory levels, shipment conditions, and equipment performance. In procurement, IoT can enable more accurate demand forecasting and better inventory management.

Robotic Process Automation (RPA): RPA automates highly repetitive, routine tasks such as data entry, invoice processing, and order tracking. This not only increases efficiency but also allows procurement teams to focus on more strategic, value-adding activities.

As these technologies mature, procurement managers who embrace them will be well-positioned to drive innovation and maintain a competitive edge in the global market.

Best Practices for Implementing Procurement Technology

Successfully integrating technology into procurement processes involves a combination of strategic planning, change management, and continuous training. Here are some best practices:

Conduct a Technology Audit:

Assess your current procurement processes and identify areas where technology can bring the most benefit. This includes evaluating your existing ERP, e_procurement, and spend analytics systems and determining if upgrades or new solutions are needed.

Define Clear Objectives:

Before investing in new technology, clearly define what you want to achieve. Are you looking to reduce cycle times, improve data accuracy, enhance supplier collaboration, or drive cost savings? Establishing clear objectives helps in selecting the right tools and measuring success.

Engage Stakeholders:

Involve key stakeholders from across the organization—such as IT, finance, operations, and legal—in the technology selection and implementation process. Their input ensures that the chosen solutions align with overall business needs and can be seamlessly integrated into existing systems.

Invest in Training and Change Management:

New technology is only as effective as the people who use it. Invest in comprehensive training programs to ensure that your procurement team is proficient in the new tools. Additionally, implement change management strategies to help staff adapt to new processes and overcome resistance.

Leverage Data for Continuous Improvement:
Once the technology is in place, use the data generated to continuously assess and improve procurement processes. Monitor key performance indicators (KPIs) such as cycle time, cost savings, supplier performance, and inventory turnover. Regularly review these metrics to identify areas for further enhancement.

Prioritize Scalability and Integration:
Choose technology solutions that are scalable and can integrate with other systems in your organization. This ensures that as your business grows, your procurement technology can grow with it, maintaining a unified, efficient supply chain management process.

The Strategic Advantage of Mastering Procurement Technology

When procurement technology is effectively mastered, it transforms the procurement function from a reactive, administrative process into a strategic, value-driven component of the organization. The benefits include:

Enhanced Efficiency:
Automation and advanced analytics streamline routine tasks and accelerate decision-making. This efficiency translates into faster procurement cycles, reduced operational costs, and improved overall performance.

Improved Supplier Relationships:
Digital tools facilitate better communication, performance tracking, and collaboration with suppliers. This leads to stronger partnerships, better negotiated contracts, and enhanced supplier performance.

Greater Visibility and Transparency:
Integrated systems provide real-time insights into procurement activities, making it easier to track spend, monitor supplier

performance, and ensure compliance. This transparency supports more informed strategic decisions and helps build trust with stakeholders.

Risk Mitigation:

Advanced analytics and predictive models enable procurement managers to identify and mitigate risks before they escalate. Whether it's supplier disruptions, market volatility, or regulatory changes, a proactive approach to risk management ensures supply chain resilience.

Long-Term Cost Savings:

By focusing on the total cost of ownership rather than just the upfront price, procurement technology helps uncover hidden costs and identify opportunities for long-term savings. This holistic approach to cost management is crucial for maintaining a competitive edge.

Innovation and Continuous Improvement:

The integration of AI, ML, and automation not only enhances current processes but also fosters a culture of continuous improvement. These technologies drive innovation by enabling procurement teams to experiment with new approaches, optimize sourcing strategies, and continuously refine their operations.

Alignment with Organizational Goals:

By leveraging procurement technology, strategic procurement managers can align their processes with the broader objectives of the organization. Whether it's achieving cost savings, improving supplier quality, or enhancing sustainability practices, technology provides the tools to ensure that procurement activities contribute directly to the organization's strategic goals.

Conclusion

Mastering procurement technology is no longer an optional endeavor for modern procurement professionals—it is a strategic imperative. Leveraging advanced tools such as ERP systems, e_procurement platforms, and spend analytics empowers procurement managers to transform their function from a series of routine transactions into a dynamic, strategic asset. Moreover, the integration of artificial intelligence, machine learning, and automation is reshaping the procurement landscape, enabling managers to make more informed decisions, predict market trends, and drive continuous improvement.

By adopting a comprehensive digital strategy, procurement managers can streamline operations, enhance supplier collaboration, and mitigate risks more effectively. The insights gained from real-time data analytics not only support better negotiation and supplier management but also ensure that procurement decisions are aligned with the long-term financial and strategic goals of the organization.

As technology continues to advance, those who invest in mastering procurement technology will be best positioned to drive sustainable competitive advantage. They will be able to anticipate changes, adapt quickly, and continuously optimize procurement processes in a way that delivers measurable value across the organization.

Ultimately, mastering procurement technology is about transforming procurement into a true strategic partner—a function that not only supports day-to-day operations but also drives innovation, enhances efficiency, and contributes significantly to the overall success of the business. Embrace the digital transformation, invest in cutting-edge tools, and continuously refine your technology strategy to unlock the full potential of strategic procurement.

By integrating technology with strategic thinking, procurement managers pave the way for a more agile, transparent, and cost-effective supply chain. The future of procurement lies in this synergy between technology and strategy—one that promises to deliver not only immediate benefits but also long-term value and sustainable growth.

This chapter has explored the critical role of procurement technology in transforming the procurement function from tactical to strategic. By leveraging ERP systems, e_procurement platforms, and spend analytics, and by harnessing the power of AI, machine learning, and automation, procurement managers can drive efficiency, innovation, and long-term value creation for their organizations.

Developing Leadership and Influence

In today's dynamic business environment, the role of the procurement professional is rapidly evolving. No longer is procurement merely a support function tasked with managing orders and negotiating contracts. Instead, procurement leaders are emerging as strategic partners within their organizations—driving change, fostering innovation, and influencing key decisions at the highest levels. Developing leadership and influence in procurement means mastering three interrelated areas: leading cross-functional teams, influencing stakeholders and gaining executive buy-in, and building a culture of strategic thinking within the procurement team. Each of these pillars is critical for transforming the procurement function from a tactical operation into a strategic asset.

Leading Cross-Functional Teams

The Need for Collaboration

One of the hallmarks of a successful procurement leader is the ability to lead cross-functional teams. In today's complex business landscape, procurement does not operate in isolation. Instead, it intersects with various functions such as finance, operations, marketing, and product development. This interdependency necessitates a collaborative approach where procurement professionals work closely with colleagues across the organization to ensure that sourcing decisions align with broader business objectives.

Effective cross-functional leadership involves creating a shared vision among diverse teams. It means aligning the goals of procurement with those of other departments—ensuring that all teams work in concert toward common strategic objectives. For example, when negotiating a contract with a supplier, a procurement leader must consider not only cost implications but also quality, delivery timelines, and the supplier's ability to innovate. By collaborating with operations and R&D, the procurement leader can ensure that these negotiations yield results that benefit the entire organization.

Strategies for Effective Cross-Functional Leadership

Establish Clear Communication Channels:
Communication is the foundation of any successful team. As a procurement leader, establishing clear and regular communication channels is essential. This can be achieved through regular meetings, shared dashboards, and collaboration tools that ensure all team members are on the same page.

Create a Shared Vision:
A compelling vision that resonates with all departments can unify efforts. This shared vision should clearly articulate how procurement contributes to the organization's strategic goals—whether that's cost savings, quality improvement, or innovation.

Foster Mutual Understanding:
Invest time in understanding the priorities and challenges of other departments. When procurement leaders appreciate the pressures and constraints faced by finance, operations, or marketing, they can tailor procurement strategies to better support these functions. Joint workshops, cross-departmental training sessions, and interdepartmental projects are excellent ways to build this understanding.

Empower Team Members:
Effective leaders delegate responsibility and empower team members to make decisions. By providing teams with the autonomy to execute parts of the procurement process, leaders foster a sense of ownership and accountability. This not only boosts team morale but also accelerates decision-making.

Implement Collaborative Technologies:

Digital collaboration tools—such as project management software, communication platforms, and data-sharing dashboards—can streamline cross-functional efforts. These technologies help break down silos and promote transparency across teams.

Case in Point: A Unified Procurement Approach

Consider a multinational manufacturing company facing supply chain disruptions. Instead of handling the crisis in isolation, the procurement leader convened a cross-functional task force comprising representatives from procurement, operations, quality assurance, and finance. Together, they analyzed data from ERP systems, assessed supplier performance, and developed a contingency plan that not only addressed the immediate disruption but also introduced strategic supplier diversification. This collaborative approach not only mitigated the risk but also resulted in long-term supplier partnerships and improved overall efficiency.

Influencing Stakeholders and Gaining Executive Buy-In

The Art of Influence in Procurement

Influence is an essential quality for procurement leaders aiming to transition from a tactical function to a strategic role. To drive change, procurement managers must effectively influence key stakeholders—including senior executives, finance leaders, and operational managers—to recognize the strategic value of procurement. Gaining executive buy-in is not simply about presenting data; it's about communicating a compelling narrative that connects procurement initiatives to overall business performance.

Techniques for Influencing Stakeholders

Build a Data-Driven Narrative:

Data is a powerful tool for influence. Use spend analytics, TCO evaluations, and supplier performance metrics to build a clear, evidence-based case for procurement initiatives. When stakeholders see quantifiable benefits, such as cost savings, efficiency improvements, and risk mitigation, they are more likely to support strategic procurement projects.

Align Procurement with Business Goals:
Ensure that procurement initiatives are directly linked to the organization's strategic objectives. For example, if a company's goal is to innovate its product line, highlight how strategic supplier partnerships and data-driven sourcing decisions can contribute to product innovation and faster time-to-market.

Leverage Success Stories:
Sharing success stories and case studies from within the organization—or from industry benchmarks—can be very persuasive. Demonstrate how previous procurement initiatives have delivered tangible benefits, such as improved quality, reduced costs, or enhanced supply chain resilience.

Engage Early and Often:
Involve stakeholders early in the procurement process. By engaging them from the outset, you build trust and foster a sense of collaboration. Regular updates and transparent communication throughout the project help maintain support and address any concerns promptly.

Develop Executive Presentations:
Craft executive-level presentations that succinctly convey the strategic impact of procurement. Use visuals, charts, and KPIs to make your case compelling and easy to understand. Tailor your message to address the priorities of each stakeholder group, whether it's cost reduction, innovation, or risk management.

Show Long-Term Vision:
Executives are more likely to support initiatives that promise

long-term benefits rather than short-term fixes. Emphasize how strategic procurement can build sustainable supplier relationships, foster innovation, and contribute to long-term business growth.

Overcoming Resistance and Building Consensus

Even with a strong data-driven case, resistance can occur. Some stakeholders might be wary of change or reluctant to invest in new procurement technologies and strategies. Here are ways to overcome resistance and build consensus:

Empathize with Concerns:
Listen to the concerns of stakeholders. Understanding their perspectives and addressing their fears—whether they are about risk, cost, or disruption—can help build trust.

Pilot Programs:
Start with a small, controlled pilot project that demonstrates the value of a new procurement strategy or technology. Once stakeholders see positive results on a small scale, they are more likely to support broader implementation.

Cross-Functional Workshops:
Organize workshops where procurement and other departments can collaboratively explore new ideas. These sessions foster a sense of shared purpose and highlight how procurement initiatives can benefit the entire organization.

Regular Reporting:
Maintain transparency by providing regular reports on procurement performance and progress. Clear, consistent communication reinforces the value of procurement initiatives and keeps stakeholders engaged.

The Importance of Executive Sponsorship

Gaining executive buy-in is not a one-time event—it's an ongoing process. Having an executive sponsor who champions procurement initiatives can make all the difference. This sponsor should be someone who understands the strategic value of procurement and is willing to advocate for necessary investments, changes, and process improvements. An executive sponsor can help navigate organizational politics, secure budget approvals, and provide the credibility needed to drive transformation.

A practical example of executive buy-in can be seen in a large retail organization that aimed to overhaul its supplier base. The procurement manager worked closely with the CFO and COO, presenting a detailed plan that highlighted cost savings, improved supplier performance, and enhanced risk management. With executive backing, the procurement initiative not only received the necessary funding but also gained the support of other departments, leading to a successful transformation of the supplier network.

Building a Culture of Strategic Thinking within the Procurement Team

Why Culture Matters

A strategic mindset does not occur overnight; it is nurtured by a culture that values continuous improvement, collaboration, and innovation. Building a culture of strategic thinking within the procurement team is essential for sustaining long-term value creation. When procurement professionals are encouraged to think beyond the day-to-day transactions and consider the broader implications of their decisions, the entire function becomes more agile, responsive, and effective.

Key Elements of a Strategic Culture

Vision and Values:
Start by establishing a clear vision for the procurement function.

This vision should articulate how procurement contributes to the organization's strategic goals and what success looks like. Aligning team values with the organization's mission fosters a sense of purpose and direction.

Continuous Learning:

Encourage a culture of continuous learning and professional development. This can be achieved through regular training sessions, workshops, industry certifications, and knowledge-sharing forums. When team members are up-to-date on the latest procurement trends and technologies, they are better equipped to drive strategic initiatives.

Innovation and Experimentation:

Foster an environment where new ideas are welcomed and experimentation is encouraged. This means creating safe spaces for team members to test new approaches, pilot innovative projects, and share insights without fear of failure. Celebrating successes and learning from failures are key to building a resilient, forward-thinking team.

Collaborative Decision-Making:

Promote collaboration within the team and across other departments. Cross-functional collaboration ensures that procurement decisions are informed by diverse perspectives and that the entire organization benefits from strategic procurement initiatives. Encourage open discussions, brainstorming sessions, and regular feedback loops.

Empowerment and Accountability:

Empower team members to take ownership of their projects and decisions. When individuals feel responsible for the outcomes of their work, they are more likely to act strategically and innovatively. At the same time, establish clear accountability measures to ensure that strategic goals are met and performance is continuously monitored.

83

Strategies for Cultivating a Strategic Procurement Culture

Leadership by Example:
As a procurement leader, demonstrate strategic thinking in your daily actions. Share your vision, explain the rationale behind strategic decisions, and involve your team in high-level planning discussions. When team members see their leader acting strategically, they are more likely to follow suit.

Set Clear Goals and KPIs:
Define clear, measurable goals that align with strategic objectives. These might include cost savings, supplier performance improvements, risk mitigation targets, and innovation metrics. Regularly review progress against these KPIs to keep the team focused and motivated.

Foster Open Communication:
Create channels for open and honest communication within the team. Encourage team members to share ideas, challenges, and successes. Regular team meetings, suggestion boxes, and online forums can facilitate this dialogue and ensure that everyone's voice is heard.

Invest in Technology and Training:
Equip your team with the latest tools and training necessary for strategic procurement. Whether it's advanced spend analytics software, AI-driven tools, or e_procurement platforms, ensure that your team is comfortable using these technologies. Continuous training not only builds competence but also reinforces the culture of innovation.

Reward and Recognize Strategic Contributions:
Develop a recognition program that rewards team members for strategic thinking, innovative ideas, and collaborative efforts. This could include bonuses, awards, or public recognition in team meetings. Recognizing and celebrating achievements

fosters a positive culture and motivates others to think strategically.

Create Cross-Functional Teams:

Encourage the formation of cross-functional project teams that include members from procurement, finance, operations, and other key departments. These teams can work on strategic projects that require diverse perspectives and help break down silos within the organization. This collaborative approach not only drives innovation but also strengthens the team's overall strategic capabilities.

Regular Strategic Reviews:

Hold periodic strategic review sessions where the procurement team evaluates current strategies, reviews market trends, and plans for the future. These sessions can be used to adjust strategies based on performance data, address emerging risks, and brainstorm new initiatives. The insights gained during these reviews are invaluable for continuous improvement.

Mentorship and Coaching:

Establish mentorship programs within the procurement team. Pair experienced procurement professionals with newer team members to transfer knowledge, build confidence, and cultivate a strategic mindset. Mentorship not only accelerates skill development but also creates a supportive environment that encourages risk-taking and innovation.

Case Study: Transforming Procurement Culture

Consider the example of a global electronics manufacturer that embarked on a journey to transform its procurement function. Initially, procurement was viewed as a cost-cutting back-office function, with little strategic impact. Recognizing the need for change, the company's new procurement director initiated a cultural transformation program aimed at building a culture of strategic thinking.

The first step was to establish a clear vision: transforming procurement into a value-creating, strategic partner that contributes to the company's innovation and growth. This vision was communicated through company-wide meetings, internal newsletters, and one-on-one sessions with team members.

Next, the director introduced regular training sessions and workshops on advanced procurement technologies, risk management, and financial analysis. The team was encouraged to embrace new tools, such as spend analytics platforms and AI-driven forecasting models, which enabled them to make data-driven decisions.

Cross-functional teams were formed to work on strategic sourcing projects that involved collaboration between procurement, R&D, and finance. These projects not only delivered significant cost savings but also resulted in innovative product improvements and stronger supplier partnerships.

Throughout the transformation, the director implemented a recognition program to celebrate strategic contributions. Team members who introduced innovative ideas or achieved exceptional results in negotiations were publicly recognized and rewarded. Over time, the procurement team evolved from a reactive, cost-focused group into a proactive, strategic unit that was deeply integrated with the company's overall business strategy.

The success of this cultural transformation was evident in the company's improved financial performance, enhanced supplier relationships, and increased ability to anticipate and mitigate risks. The case study highlights that building a culture of strategic thinking within the procurement team is not only possible but also essential for long-term success.

Conclusion

Developing leadership and influence within the procurement function is a multifaceted journey that requires a focus on three critical areas:

leading cross-functional teams, influencing stakeholders and gaining executive buy-in, and building a culture of strategic thinking within the procurement team. By mastering these areas, procurement managers can transform their role from one of administrative support to that of a strategic leader who drives innovation, efficiency, and long-term value for the organization.

Leading cross-functional teams ensures that procurement initiatives are aligned with the broader goals of the organization. It requires strong communication, collaboration, and the ability to foster a shared vision among diverse groups. Influencing stakeholders and gaining executive buy-in are essential for securing the necessary support and resources to implement strategic initiatives. This involves building a compelling, data-driven narrative that resonates with senior leaders and addresses their strategic priorities. Finally, building a culture of strategic thinking within the procurement team ensures that every member is aligned with the organization's long-term objectives. It involves creating an environment that values continuous learning, innovation, and collaboration.

By investing in professional development, leveraging advanced technologies, and adopting best practices for leadership, procurement managers can position themselves—and their teams—as indispensable strategic partners within their organizations. This transformation is not just about enhancing the procurement function; it is about driving the overall success of the business. With strong leadership and influence, procurement can move from being a back-office support function to a critical driver of innovation, efficiency, and sustainable competitive advantage.

Embrace the journey of developing leadership and influence. Build the skills, foster the culture, and lead with purpose. In doing so, you will not only transform your procurement team but also significantly contribute to the long-term success and resilience of your organization.

This chapter has explored the multifaceted approach to developing leadership and influence in procurement, emphasizing the importance of cross-functional collaboration, stakeholder engagement, and a culture of strategic thinking. By mastering these competencies, procurement leaders can elevate their role, drive innovation, and ensure that procurement is a true strategic partner within the organization.

Part 3: Implementing Strategic Procurement Practices

Strategic Sourcing: The Foundation for Value Creation

Strategic sourcing is the process of developing sourcing strategies that align procurement activities with the organization's broader business goals. It goes beyond simply negotiating the lowest price—it considers quality, delivery, innovation, and long-term supplier partnerships.

Defining Strategic Sourcing

Strategic sourcing is a holistic, data-driven process. It begins by analyzing an organization's spend, understanding market dynamics, and evaluating supplier capabilities. The objective is to establish a sourcing strategy that not only reduces costs but also creates value by optimizing the total cost of ownership (TCO). A strategic sourcing approach ensures that procurement decisions are aligned with business priorities and that suppliers are chosen based on their ability to support long-term objectives.

Key components of strategic sourcing include:

> **Spend Analysis:** An in-depth review of historical spend data to identify trends, inefficiencies, and opportunities for consolidation.

> **Market Research:** Understanding the supplier market, including trends, risks, and emerging innovations, which informs negotiation strategies and supplier selection.

> **Supplier Evaluation:** Assessing potential suppliers based on criteria that include cost, quality, capacity, innovation capability, and risk.

Contract Negotiation: Developing contracts that are flexible, long-term, and mutually beneficial, ensuring value creation throughout the supplier relationship.

Continuous Improvement: Implementing feedback mechanisms to track supplier performance and adjust sourcing strategies as market conditions evolve.

Steps to Implement Strategic Sourcing

Assess Current Spend and Needs:
Begin by collecting and analyzing spend data to understand where money is being spent, the key categories involved, and the business requirements behind each purchase. This step lays the groundwork for identifying areas with high potential for savings or process improvements.

Conduct Market and Supplier Research:
Use market intelligence tools and spend analytics to assess the competitive landscape. Understand what suppliers offer, evaluate their capabilities, and benchmark prices. This research informs which suppliers are best positioned to meet current and future needs.

Develop a Sourcing Strategy:
Based on the spend analysis and market research, create a comprehensive sourcing strategy that outlines objectives, preferred suppliers, and negotiation tactics. This strategy should include a clear roadmap for supplier selection, risk mitigation, and continuous performance review.

Negotiate and Formalize Contracts:
Engage in negotiations that leverage data and market insights to secure favorable terms. Develop contracts that include performance metrics, risk-sharing provisions, and mechanisms for continuous improvement.

Monitor and Review:
Once contracts are in place, monitor supplier performance using KPIs such as quality, delivery, cost savings, and innovation. Regular reviews ensure that the sourcing strategy remains aligned with business objectives and can be adjusted in response to changes in the market or business needs.

Real-World Example

A multinational electronics manufacturer implemented a strategic sourcing initiative to revamp its supplier base. By analyzing historical spend and conducting market research, the company identified that a handful of suppliers were responsible for a large percentage of spend but were delivering inconsistent quality. The procurement team developed a new sourcing strategy that emphasized long-term partnerships, improved quality controls, and a focus on TCO rather than merely the lowest price. Through data-driven negotiations and flexible contract terms, the company secured better quality components at a competitive cost, reduced supplier-related disruptions, and ultimately drove innovation in product development.

Category Management and Segmentation

Category management is a strategic approach to organizing procurement activities by grouping similar items or services into categories. This method enables procurement professionals to manage each category as a distinct business unit, focusing on cost reduction, quality improvement, and risk mitigation.

Understanding Category Management

Category management involves segmenting spend into distinct groups based on factors such as product type, usage, supplier market conditions, and strategic importance. By doing so, organizations can tailor procurement strategies for each category, optimizing the overall value derived from their spend.

Key benefits of category management include:

Focused Strategies: Tailored strategies for different categories lead to more effective supplier negotiations and improved cost savings.

Risk Mitigation: Segmentation allows for better identification of category-specific risks and the development of targeted mitigation plans.

Enhanced Collaboration: Cross-functional teams can work together on category-specific strategies, ensuring that procurement activities align with both internal needs and market realities.

Continuous Improvement: Regular reviews of category performance help uncover opportunities for consolidation, innovation, and process improvements.

Implementing Category Management

Data Collection and Analysis:
Start by gathering data on all procurement spend. Use advanced analytics to segment this spend into categories. Common categories might include raw materials, indirect spend (such as office supplies), services, and capital expenditures.

Define Category Objectives:
For each category, establish clear objectives that align with overall business goals. This might include cost savings targets, quality improvements, or risk reduction goals. Defining these objectives helps in developing a tailored strategy for each category.

Develop Category Strategies:
Develop strategies that address the unique challenges and opportunities within each category. This includes selecting the

right suppliers, negotiating long-term contracts, and establishing performance metrics. Utilize frameworks such as the Kraljic Matrix to assess the strategic importance and risk associated with each category.

Implement and Monitor:
Put category strategies into action, ensuring that procurement teams and relevant stakeholders are aligned. Use category-specific KPIs to monitor performance and adjust strategies as needed. Continuous improvement is essential—regularly review the effectiveness of category strategies and make data-driven adjustments.

Segmentation: Focusing on the Right Areas

Segmentation is critical to ensure that each category is managed according to its unique characteristics. It allows procurement professionals to prioritize categories that have the greatest impact on the organization's performance and strategic goals.

Effective segmentation involves:

Assessing Spend Volume:
Identify which categories constitute the highest percentage of spend and focus efforts on these high-impact areas.

Evaluating Strategic Importance:
Beyond cost, assess which categories are critical for the organization's competitiveness and innovation. Categories tied to key products or services often require more strategic attention.

Analyzing Market Dynamics:
Understand the supplier market for each category. Some categories might be highly competitive, while others could be dominated by a few key players. This insight helps in tailoring negotiation and sourcing strategies.

Case Study: Category Management in Action

A global automotive company implemented category management to revamp its procurement strategy for components. By segmenting spend into categories such as electronic components, mechanical parts, and raw materials, the procurement team was able to develop targeted strategies for each area. They used the Kraljic Matrix to identify which categories were strategic and required long-term supplier partnerships versus those where cost was the primary driver. The focused approach led to better supplier negotiations, reduced lead times, and enhanced overall quality. In the long run, the company realized significant cost savings and improved supply chain resilience.

Supplier Relationship Management (SRM) and Collaboration

Supplier Relationship Management (SRM) is a key component of strategic procurement. It focuses on building and maintaining strong, collaborative relationships with suppliers to drive value, foster innovation, and mitigate risks.

The Importance of SRM

In a strategic procurement framework, suppliers are not seen as isolated vendors but as partners in the value chain. Effective SRM:

Enhances Collaboration:
Through ongoing communication and joint initiatives, organizations and suppliers can work together to innovate, streamline processes, and improve product quality.

Improves Supplier Performance:
Regular performance reviews, feedback sessions, and collaboration on continuous improvement initiatives help ensure that suppliers meet or exceed contractual expectations.

Reduces Risks:
Strong supplier relationships make it easier to address issues

quickly, whether they are related to quality, delivery, or compliance. A collaborative approach also facilitates better contingency planning and risk mitigation.

Drives Cost Savings:
Long-term partnerships often lead to better negotiated terms, volume discounts, and lower total costs of ownership.

Strategies for Effective SRM

Establish Clear Communication:
Open and regular communication is essential. Use technology platforms and regular meetings to ensure both parties are aligned on objectives, performance expectations, and upcoming challenges.

Set Performance Metrics:
Develop and implement supplier scorecards that track key performance indicators such as quality, delivery, cost, and innovation. These metrics provide a basis for ongoing evaluation and improvement.

Foster Joint Innovation:
Collaborate with suppliers on research and development initiatives. Joint innovation projects can lead to new product developments, process improvements, and shared cost savings.

Create Long-Term Partnerships:
Move away from one-off transactions and focus on building long-term relationships. Long-term contracts and strategic alliances provide stability and mutual benefits that extend beyond immediate cost savings.

Leverage Technology:
Use SRM software to manage supplier information, track performance, and facilitate communication. These tools help ensure transparency and enable data-driven decision-making.

Regular Supplier Reviews:
Conduct periodic performance reviews with key suppliers. Use these reviews to discuss successes, identify areas for improvement, and adjust strategies as needed. A collaborative approach ensures that issues are addressed before they escalate.

Real-World Example

A leading pharmaceutical company restructured its supplier relationship management approach by implementing an SRM platform. The platform allowed the company to track supplier performance in real time, monitor quality metrics, and schedule regular performance review meetings. Over time, the company was able to build deeper partnerships with its suppliers, resulting in improved product quality, reduced lead times, and lower overall costs. Joint innovation projects led to the development of new formulations and process improvements that provided a competitive advantage in a rapidly changing market.

Sustainable and Ethical Sourcing Practices

Sustainability and ethics have become increasingly critical in procurement. Today, organizations are not only evaluated on cost and quality but also on their environmental impact, social responsibility, and adherence to ethical standards.

Defining Sustainable and Ethical Sourcing

Sustainable sourcing is the practice of procuring goods and services in a way that minimizes environmental impact, supports fair labor practices, and promotes long-term ecological balance. Ethical sourcing goes hand-in-hand with sustainability by ensuring that procurement decisions are made in accordance with moral and ethical standards, avoiding suppliers involved in exploitative practices or those that harm the environment.

Key elements of sustainable and ethical sourcing include:

Environmental Impact:
Evaluating suppliers based on their environmental practices, such as reducing emissions, waste management, and resource conservation.

Social Responsibility:
Ensuring suppliers adhere to fair labor practices, promote workplace safety, and support local communities.

Transparency and Traceability:
Maintaining clear records of the supply chain to ensure that every stage of the procurement process meets ethical standards.

Compliance with Regulations:
Adhering to local, national, and international regulations related to environmental protection, labor rights, and ethical business practices.

Implementing Sustainable Sourcing Strategies

To successfully integrate sustainable sourcing into procurement practices, organizations should adopt the following strategies:

Supplier Sustainability Assessments:
Evaluate potential suppliers not just on cost and quality but also on their sustainability practices. Use sustainability scorecards and audits to assess environmental impact, labor conditions, and ethical practices.

Set Clear Sustainability Goals:
Establish measurable sustainability targets for procurement. These goals might include reducing carbon emissions, increasing the percentage of spend on sustainable products, or ensuring that a certain percentage of suppliers meet specific ethical standards.

Integrate Sustainability into Supplier Contracts:

Incorporate sustainability clauses into contracts to ensure that suppliers commit to sustainable practices. This can include requirements for environmental reporting, adherence to social responsibility standards, or participation in sustainability initiatives.

Collaborate on Innovation:

Work with suppliers to develop innovative solutions that enhance sustainability. This could involve joint R&D projects, sharing best practices, or co-investing in green technologies that reduce environmental impact and improve efficiency.

Monitor and Report Progress:

Use advanced analytics and reporting tools to monitor sustainability performance across the supply chain. Regular reporting ensures accountability and allows organizations to make data-driven adjustments to their procurement strategies.

Engage Stakeholders:

Involve internal stakeholders, including senior leadership and cross-functional teams, in setting sustainability priorities. Gaining executive buy-in is crucial for ensuring that sustainable sourcing practices are supported at all levels of the organization.

Benefits of Sustainable and Ethical Sourcing

Implementing sustainable and ethical sourcing practices delivers numerous benefits:

Enhanced Brand Reputation:

Companies that prioritize sustainability and ethics build trust with consumers, investors, and other stakeholders, enhancing their brand reputation.

Long-Term Cost Savings:
Sustainable practices often lead to efficiencies and cost reductions over time, such as reduced waste and lower energy consumption.

Risk Mitigation:
Ethical sourcing minimizes risks related to labor disputes, regulatory fines, and reputational damage. It also helps secure a more resilient supply chain.

Innovation Opportunities:
Collaborating on sustainability initiatives can drive innovation, resulting in new products or processes that provide competitive advantages.

Regulatory Compliance:
Adhering to sustainability and ethical standards ensures compliance with evolving regulations, reducing the risk of legal issues.

Positive Social Impact:
Ethical sourcing supports fair labor practices and community development, contributing to broader social responsibility goals.

Case Study: Sustainable Sourcing in Practice

A global apparel brand recognized that its traditional sourcing practices were not meeting the company's sustainability goals. The procurement team embarked on a comprehensive sustainable sourcing initiative that began with a full audit of its supplier base. They used sustainability scorecards to assess each supplier's environmental and social performance and then re-segmented their supplier portfolio to prioritize those that met strict sustainability criteria.

The team renegotiated contracts to include sustainability clauses, required regular environmental audits, and even collaborated with suppliers to implement new, eco-friendly production processes. Over a period of two years, the brand reduced its carbon footprint by 25%, improved product quality through innovative materials, and enhanced its brand image by marketing its commitment to ethical practices. This transformation not only resulted in long-term cost savings but also positioned the company as a leader in sustainable fashion.

Integrating Strategic Procurement Practices: A Holistic Approach

Implementing strategic procurement practices involves a holistic approach where each component—strategic sourcing, category management, supplier relationship management, and sustainable sourcing—interlocks to form a cohesive strategy. This integration ensures that procurement activities are not only aligned with immediate business needs but also contribute to long-term organizational goals.

The Interplay Between Strategic Sourcing and Category Management

Strategic sourcing lays the groundwork for effective procurement by identifying opportunities, negotiating favorable terms, and establishing long-term supplier partnerships. Category management takes this a step further by organizing spend into distinct categories, allowing procurement professionals to apply targeted strategies based on the unique characteristics of each category. Together, these practices create a structured framework that drives both cost efficiency and value creation.

For instance, in a complex category such as raw materials for manufacturing, strategic sourcing might focus on negotiating long-term contracts and leveraging volume discounts. Meanwhile, category management ensures that the sourcing strategy is continuously optimized through regular market analysis, risk assessments, and supplier performance reviews.

Enhancing Supplier Relationships Through Collaboration

A critical component of strategic procurement is the cultivation of robust supplier relationships. When procurement teams work closely with suppliers, they not only secure better pricing and terms but also drive innovation and improve quality. Supplier relationship management (SRM) involves continuous collaboration, regular performance reviews, and joint problem-solving initiatives. This collaborative approach transforms suppliers from mere vendors into strategic partners who share in the risks and rewards of procurement decisions.

Embedding Sustainability into Procurement Strategies

Sustainable and ethical sourcing practices are no longer optional—they are a necessity in today's business environment. By embedding sustainability into procurement strategies, organizations can ensure that their supplier base adheres to ethical standards and environmental best practices. This integration not only mitigates risks but also enhances the organization's reputation and drives long-term value.

A comprehensive sustainable sourcing strategy involves rigorous supplier assessments, clear sustainability targets, and continuous monitoring of performance. It requires collaboration with suppliers, investment in green technologies, and a commitment to transparency and ethical practices. By adopting these practices, procurement professionals can drive a cultural shift within the organization that prioritizes long-term environmental and social responsibility alongside financial performance.

Conclusion

Implementing strategic procurement practices is a transformative journey that reshapes the procurement function into a strategic driver of organizational success. Through strategic sourcing, procurement managers identify and engage with the best suppliers, leveraging data and market insights to secure favorable contracts and optimize spend.

102

Category management and segmentation enable the procurement function to focus on high-impact areas, ensuring that every dollar spent aligns with the organization's strategic goals. Robust supplier relationship management fosters collaboration and innovation, turning suppliers into long-term partners who contribute to continuous improvement and risk mitigation. Meanwhile, sustainable and ethical sourcing practices ensure that procurement decisions not only drive financial performance but also support environmental and social responsibility.

A holistic approach that integrates these elements empowers procurement professionals to move from a reactive, tactical function to a proactive, strategic role. The benefits are multifold: enhanced cost efficiency, improved supplier performance, reduced risk, and a stronger organizational reputation. In today's competitive and rapidly evolving market, the ability to implement strategic procurement practices is a key differentiator that can lead to sustained competitive advantage.

As you continue on your journey from tactical to strategic procurement, remember that the implementation of these practices requires a blend of analytical rigor, collaborative leadership, and a steadfast commitment to continuous improvement. Embrace the opportunities presented by advanced technologies, data-driven insights, and a culture of sustainability. By doing so, you not only enhance your own capabilities but also elevate the entire procurement function to a level where it becomes an indispensable strategic asset within your organization.

In summary, the shift to strategic procurement practices is not just about saving money—it's about creating value. It's about transforming procurement from a series of isolated transactions into a cohesive, integrated function that drives innovation, efficiency, and long-term success. Embrace strategic sourcing, master category management, cultivate strong supplier relationships, and commit to sustainable and ethical sourcing. The future of procurement lies in these strategic practices, and by implementing them, you pave the way for a more resilient, innovative, and profitable organization..

Driving Innovation Through Procurement

Innovation is no longer confined to product development or R&D departments. In today's rapidly evolving business landscape, procurement has emerged as a key driver of innovation, transforming the traditional role of procurement from a cost-cutting function to a strategic enabler of growth and competitive advantage. By adopting innovative procurement practices, organizations can unlock new sources of value, optimize their supply chains, and respond agilely to market disruptions. This chapter explores three critical dimensions of driving innovation through procurement:

Identifying Opportunities for Innovation in the Supply Chain

Partnering with Suppliers to Co-Create Value

Leveraging Market Trends and Disruptions

Each of these areas is essential for integrating innovation into procurement practices and ultimately transforming the procurement function into a strategic asset.

Identifying Opportunities for Innovation in the Supply Chain

Understanding the Supply Chain Landscape

To drive innovation, procurement leaders must have a comprehensive understanding of the supply chain. This means not only knowing where every component comes from but also recognizing inefficiencies, bottlenecks, and areas ripe for improvement. A thorough supply chain analysis—leveraging data analytics and market research—can reveal hidden opportunities. For example, by analyzing historical spend data and supplier performance metrics, procurement teams can identify segments with high variability in cost or quality, signaling a potential opportunity for innovation.

Leveraging Data Analytics

Modern procurement functions increasingly rely on advanced analytics to uncover patterns and trends. Data-driven insights can identify areas where technological improvements or process innovations could significantly enhance efficiency. Tools such as spend analytics platforms and ERP systems enable procurement professionals to monitor supplier performance, track inventory levels, and analyze transactional data to spot discrepancies and inefficiencies. These insights often reveal opportunities to streamline processes, consolidate suppliers, or adopt new technologies that drive innovation.

For instance, an organization may discover that frequent late deliveries are not only affecting production schedules but also increasing costs. In response, the procurement team might explore innovative logistics solutions or work with suppliers to implement more advanced tracking and forecasting systems. The key is to transform raw data into actionable insights that directly inform innovation strategies.

Process Re-engineering and Lean Principles

Innovation in procurement also comes from re-engineering existing processes. By adopting lean methodologies, procurement managers can identify and eliminate waste, reduce cycle times, and improve overall efficiency. Lean principles encourage continuous improvement and can be applied to procurement workflows to minimize delays and reduce redundancy. This process re-engineering not only cuts costs but also frees up resources to focus on strategic, innovative initiatives.

Embracing Digital Technologies

The digital revolution has introduced a myriad of technologies that are transforming supply chain management. Cloud-based platforms, mobile applications, and the Internet of Things (IoT) enable real-time tracking and improved visibility across the supply chain. Procurement professionals should continuously scan for technological trends and assess how emerging solutions can be integrated into their operations to drive innovation.

For example, IoT devices can monitor the condition of goods during transportation, providing data that helps predict maintenance needs or optimize inventory management. Similarly, digital twin technology can simulate supply chain operations to forecast the impact of potential changes before they are implemented. These innovations create an environment where procurement is continuously evolving and improving.

Partnering with Suppliers to Co-Create Value

Shifting from Transactional to Collaborative Relationships

Historically, procurement was largely transactional—focused solely on negotiating the lowest price. Today, the best procurement practices emphasize strategic partnerships with suppliers. When suppliers are treated as collaborative partners rather than mere vendors, the potential for co-creating value increases dramatically. This collaborative mindset fosters an environment where both parties are invested in the success of the relationship and are more willing to share ideas, risks, and innovations.

Developing Joint Innovation Initiatives

One of the most effective ways to drive innovation through procurement is by launching joint innovation initiatives with suppliers. This can take various forms, from co-developing new products and technologies to improving existing processes. For instance, a company might work with a supplier to redesign packaging that reduces waste and lowers transportation costs. Such initiatives not only lead to cost savings but also enhance product quality and sustainability.

Successful joint innovation requires a clear framework for collaboration. Both parties should agree on mutual objectives, define success metrics, and establish open communication channels. This partnership should be built on trust, transparency, and a shared commitment to long-term value creation. Tools like collaborative digital platforms can facilitate regular brainstorming sessions, virtual workshops, and performance reviews that keep innovation initiatives on track.

Contractual Flexibility for Innovation

Contracts are often seen as static documents that lock parties into fixed terms. However, modern procurement strategies advocate for flexible contracts that allow for continuous improvement and innovation. Including innovation clauses in contracts can incentivize suppliers to invest in research and development, share technological advancements, or even implement process improvements. Flexible contracts can also provide mechanisms for regular review and adjustment based on performance data, ensuring that the supplier relationship remains dynamic and responsive to changing market conditions.

Building Trust and Long-Term Partnerships

For co-creation of value to occur, procurement leaders must invest in building long-term relationships based on trust. Trust is built through consistent, transparent communication and a commitment to shared success. Regular performance reviews, joint strategic planning sessions, and open forums for feedback help foster a collaborative environment where suppliers feel valued and motivated to innovate.

An example of this approach in action is seen in the automotive industry, where manufacturers work closely with key suppliers to develop innovative components and technologies. By engaging suppliers early in the product development cycle, manufacturers can ensure that new parts are designed with efficiency, performance, and cost in mind—leading to better overall products and a more resilient supply chain.

Leveraging Market Trends and Disruptions

Monitoring and Anticipating Market Changes

The modern procurement landscape is marked by rapid changes and disruptions—from economic fluctuations and technological advances to geopolitical events and environmental challenges. To drive innovation, procurement leaders must stay ahead of these trends and be prepared to adapt quickly. Leveraging market intelligence and predictive analytics enables procurement teams to anticipate shifts in demand, supplier capabilities, and market dynamics.

For example, fluctuations in commodity prices or changes in regulatory environments can have a significant impact on procurement decisions. By using advanced analytics to monitor these trends, procurement managers can adjust their strategies in real time—whether that means renegotiating contracts, diversifying the supplier base, or even developing new sourcing strategies.

Capitalizing on Disruptions

Market disruptions, though challenging, can also be a catalyst for innovation. Disruptions force organizations to rethink their supply chain strategies, adopt new technologies, and explore alternative sourcing options. In times of disruption, agility is key. Procurement leaders who can rapidly pivot their strategies and embrace innovative solutions will be better positioned to mitigate risks and capitalize on new opportunities.

Consider the global disruptions caused by the COVID-19 pandemic, which forced many organizations to reevaluate their supply chains. Companies that quickly adopted digital tools, diversified their supplier base, and embraced remote collaboration were able to maintain continuity and even discover new efficiencies. Disruptions often highlight vulnerabilities in existing processes, providing a clear impetus for innovation and improvement.

Strategic Use of Technology in Disruption Management

Advanced technologies, such as AI and machine learning, play a pivotal role in helping procurement leaders navigate market disruptions. These technologies can analyze vast amounts of data in real time, forecast potential disruptions, and suggest proactive measures. For instance, AI-driven predictive analytics can alert procurement teams to potential supply shortages or quality issues before they become critical, allowing for timely interventions.

Furthermore, blockchain technology offers enhanced transparency and traceability, which can be crucial during disruptions. By providing an immutable record of transactions, blockchain can help verify the authenticity of goods, track shipments, and ensure compliance with regulatory requirements. This level of transparency is especially valuable in times of uncertainty when trust and accuracy are paramount.

Case Study: Innovating Amid Disruption

A global consumer electronics company faced significant supply chain disruptions due to geopolitical tensions and trade restrictions. Rather than relying on traditional sourcing methods, the company leveraged its procurement analytics platform to monitor global market trends and identify alternative suppliers in emerging markets. By integrating AI-driven predictive analytics, the procurement team was able to forecast potential supply shortages and proactively adjust its sourcing strategy.

The company also initiated joint innovation projects with key suppliers to develop new materials and components that were less vulnerable to supply chain disruptions. These initiatives not only helped mitigate the immediate risks but also resulted in long-term cost savings and enhanced product quality. The successful navigation of these challenges underscored the importance of leveraging market trends and disruptions as opportunities for innovation.

Integrating Innovation into Procurement Strategy

Driving innovation through procurement is not about sporadic, isolated initiatives; it is about embedding a culture of innovation into the very fabric of the procurement function. This requires a strategic approach that integrates technology, supplier collaboration, and market intelligence into every stage of the procurement process.

Fostering a Culture of Innovation

A culture that values innovation encourages every member of the procurement team to think creatively and seek continuous improvement. This involves:

Encouraging Idea Sharing: Create forums or regular brainstorming sessions where team members can propose innovative ideas and discuss potential improvements.

Rewarding Innovation: Recognize and reward innovative initiatives that lead to measurable improvements, whether they are cost savings, process efficiencies, or enhanced supplier collaboration.

Investing in Training: Provide training on the latest procurement technologies, innovation methodologies, and industry trends to empower the team to think outside the box.

Setting Ambitious Goals: Establish strategic objectives that push the boundaries of traditional procurement, such as implementing new digital tools or launching joint innovation projects with suppliers.

Measuring Innovation Success

To ensure that innovation efforts yield tangible results, it is essential to establish metrics and KPIs that track progress. These might include:

Cost Savings: Quantify savings achieved through innovative sourcing strategies or process improvements.

Time-to-Market: Measure how innovation initiatives reduce lead times or accelerate product development cycles.

Supplier Performance: Track improvements in supplier quality, delivery, and collaboration resulting from joint innovation projects.

Return on Investment (ROI): Assess the financial impact of innovation initiatives to ensure they deliver a positive ROI.

Adoption Rate: Monitor the adoption of new technologies or processes within the procurement team and across the organization.

Conclusion

Driving innovation through procurement is a transformative journey that reshapes the function from a traditional, transactional role into a strategic powerhouse capable of delivering long-term value. By identifying opportunities for innovation in the supply chain, partnering with suppliers to co-create value, and leveraging market trends and disruptions, procurement leaders can unlock new sources of competitive advantage and drive sustainable growth.

Strategic sourcing lays the foundation by using data-driven insights to uncover inefficiencies and optimize supplier selection. Category management and segmentation further refine this approach by allowing procurement teams to focus on high-impact areas. Supplier relationship management (SRM) transforms suppliers into collaborative partners who share in the innovation journey, while sustainable and ethical sourcing ensures that these innovations are responsible and aligned with broader corporate values.

Moreover, embracing advanced technologies—such as AI, machine learning, blockchain, and IoT—enables procurement teams to predict market changes, manage disruptions, and continuously improve their processes. The integration of these technologies not only enhances operational efficiency but also supports proactive, strategic decision-making.

Ultimately, driving innovation through procurement is about creating a culture that encourages creativity, collaboration, and continuous improvement. It requires a holistic approach that aligns procurement strategies with organizational goals, empowers teams with the latest tools and technologies, and fosters strong, mutually beneficial relationships with suppliers. By embracing this innovative mindset, procurement professionals can transform their function into a critical driver of business success, delivering measurable value and ensuring long-term competitive advantage.

As you work to implement these strategic procurement practices, remember that innovation is not a one-off project but a continuous journey. It is the result of persistent effort, open collaboration, and the willingness to challenge conventional approaches. By integrating innovation into every aspect of procurement, you will not only reduce costs and mitigate risks but also drive sustainable growth and build a resilient, future-ready organization.

Embrace the power of innovation in procurement, and let it be the force that propels your organization into a new era of efficiency, creativity, and strategic excellence.

This chapter has explored the multifaceted process of driving innovation through procurement—from identifying opportunities in the supply chain and partnering with suppliers for co-creation, to leveraging market trends and disruptions as catalysts for transformation. By embedding innovation into procurement strategy, organizations can unlock new value, enhance supplier performance, and ensure long-term success in a rapidly changing business environment.

Risk Management and Resilience

In a global marketplace marked by volatility, uncertainty, complexity, and ambiguity (VUCA), a robust risk management and resilience strategy is essential for procurement functions to thrive. In this chapter, we explore how strategic procurement managers can identify and mitigate supply chain risks, build resilient procurement strategies, and implement scenario planning and contingency strategies. By adopting these practices, organizations can safeguard against disruptions, enhance supply chain stability, and secure long-term business success.

Identifying and Mitigating Supply Chain Risks

Understanding Supply Chain Risks

Supply chain risks come in many forms. They can stem from external factors—such as geopolitical instability, natural disasters, or economic downturns—or internal factors, including supplier financial instability, quality issues, or logistical failures. Effective risk management starts with a comprehensive understanding of these risks, which enables procurement professionals to develop targeted strategies to mitigate them.

Key types of risks include:

Operational Risks: These involve disruptions in the day-to-day activities of the supply chain, such as production delays, quality control failures, and logistical bottlenecks.

Financial Risks: Fluctuations in currency exchange rates, price volatility, and supplier insolvency can have significant financial implications.

114

Strategic Risks: Changes in market conditions, evolving customer demands, or competitive pressures that may render existing sourcing strategies obsolete.

Compliance Risks: Regulatory changes, non-adherence to ethical standards, and environmental or labor law violations that can expose the organization to legal liabilities and reputational damage.

Environmental and Social Risks: These include the impacts of climate change, natural disasters, and the sustainability practices of suppliers.

Tools and Techniques for Risk Identification

To effectively manage these risks, procurement managers should adopt a systematic approach:

Risk Assessments and Audits: Regular risk assessments help identify potential vulnerabilities in the supply chain. Audits of supplier performance, financial health, and compliance with regulatory standards are critical.

Data Analytics and Monitoring: Advanced analytics tools enable procurement teams to monitor real-time data from ERP systems, spend analytics platforms, and supplier scorecards. These tools can flag anomalies or early indicators of risk.

Supplier Segmentation: Using frameworks such as the Kraljic Matrix, suppliers can be categorized based on their strategic importance and risk levels. High-risk, high-impact suppliers require closer scrutiny and more robust contingency planning.

Market Intelligence: Staying abreast of global and regional market trends, economic forecasts, and geopolitical developments provides context for risk assessment. Leveraging external data sources and industry reports is essential.

Mitigation Strategies

Once risks have been identified, the next step is to develop and implement mitigation strategies. Some effective risk mitigation strategies include:

Diversification of Suppliers: Avoid over-reliance on a single supplier by diversifying your supplier base. This reduces vulnerability to disruptions from any one source.

Long-Term Supplier Relationships: Establishing long-term partnerships with suppliers can foster greater collaboration, transparency, and mutual risk-sharing. Strong relationships often lead to better communication and quicker resolution of issues.

Flexible Contracts: Incorporate risk-sharing clauses in contracts, such as price adjustment mechanisms, performance guarantees, or options for renegotiation, to accommodate unexpected changes.

Inventory Management Strategies: Maintaining safety stock or buffer inventories can provide a cushion against supply interruptions, particularly in critical categories.

Technology Integration: Utilize digital tools, such as AI-driven predictive analytics and blockchain for transparency, to monitor supplier performance and detect early signs of potential disruption.

Regular Supplier Audits and Performance Reviews: Continuous monitoring and performance evaluation of suppliers ensure that risks are identified early and addressed promptly.

Building a Resilient Procurement Strategy

Resilience in procurement means the ability to absorb shocks, recover quickly from disruptions, and adapt to changing circumstances. A resilient procurement strategy not only mitigates risks but also ensures that the organization can continue operating under adverse conditions.

Characteristics of a Resilient Procurement Strategy

Flexibility:
A flexible procurement strategy can adjust quickly to changes. This may involve having multiple sourcing options, scalable inventory solutions, or the ability to shift between suppliers as needed.

Redundancy:
Building redundancy into the supply chain—such as having backup suppliers or alternative production sites—ensures that if one part of the supply chain fails, another can quickly take its place.

Visibility and Transparency:
A resilient strategy depends on real-time visibility into every aspect of the supply chain. Integrated systems that provide transparency into supplier performance, inventory levels, and logistical operations enable quicker decision-making and more effective responses to disruptions.

Proactive Risk Management:
Rather than simply reacting to disruptions, a resilient strategy anticipates risks through predictive analytics and scenario planning. Proactive measures, such as diversifying suppliers and establishing flexible contracts, are key to long-term resilience.

Collaboration and Communication:
Effective collaboration with suppliers and internal stakeholders is crucial. Open lines of communication allow for rapid

response to issues, shared problem-solving, and joint risk management initiatives.

Strategic Elements of Resilience

Building resilience requires a combination of strategic planning and tactical execution. Key elements include:

Diversification:
Strategic diversification of suppliers, production locations, and transportation routes reduces dependency on any single source. This not only minimizes risk but can also lead to cost efficiencies through competitive sourcing.

Investment in Technology:
Advanced technologies such as AI, machine learning, and IoT provide the data and insights necessary for proactive risk management. These tools can forecast potential disruptions and help organizations adjust their strategies in real time.

Sustainable Sourcing:
Emphasizing sustainability in sourcing practices contributes to long-term resilience. Suppliers that adhere to ethical and environmental standards are less likely to be disrupted by regulatory changes or reputational risks.

Scenario Planning:
Scenario planning involves mapping out potential future scenarios and developing contingency plans for each. This exercise helps organizations prepare for a range of possibilities—from minor supply chain hiccups to major geopolitical disruptions.

Business Continuity Planning:
A comprehensive business continuity plan ensures that critical operations can continue in the face of disruptions. For procurement, this may include maintaining emergency

inventory levels, establishing alternative supply routes, and having backup contracts in place.

Implementing Resilient Procurement Strategies

Conduct a Comprehensive Risk Assessment:

Start by assessing the vulnerabilities in your current procurement processes. Identify high-risk categories, assess supplier risks, and analyze the potential impact of disruptions. Use data analytics and market intelligence to gain a clear picture of where resilience improvements are most needed.

Develop a Resilience Roadmap:

Create a detailed plan that outlines specific initiatives to enhance procurement resilience. This roadmap should include diversification strategies, technology investments, and contingency plans. Establish clear timelines and milestones for each initiative.

Establish Backup Plans and Redundancies:

For critical supply categories, identify alternative suppliers and create backup agreements. Maintain strategic buffer inventories and consider geographical diversification to reduce the impact of regional disruptions.

Invest in Advanced Technologies:

Leverage AI and machine learning to monitor real-time data and predict potential disruptions. Implement IoT devices to track the condition and movement of goods, and consider blockchain for enhanced transparency and traceability in supplier transactions.

Enhance Communication and Collaboration:

Develop formal communication channels with key suppliers and internal stakeholders. Regularly schedule risk review meetings, establish a crisis management team, and ensure that everyone is aware of the contingency plans. Collaboration tools and digital platforms can help facilitate this communication.

Train and Develop Your Team:

A resilient procurement strategy depends on a team that is well-trained in risk management and contingency planning. Invest in training programs that enhance your team's skills in predictive analytics, scenario planning, and crisis management. Encourage a culture of continuous improvement and adaptability.

Monitor and Review Performance:

Establish key performance indicators (KPIs) related to supply chain resilience. These might include supplier performance ratings, delivery lead times, and recovery times from disruptions. Regularly review these metrics to assess the effectiveness of your resilience strategies and make data-driven adjustments.

Scenario Planning and Contingency Strategies

The Importance of Scenario Planning

Scenario planning is a proactive approach that prepares organizations for a range of potential future conditions. In procurement, scenario planning involves envisioning various disruption scenarios—such as natural disasters, economic downturns, supplier insolvency, or geopolitical crises—and developing strategies to address them. This exercise helps ensure that the procurement function is not caught off guard and that there are predefined responses to mitigate the impact of disruptions.

Steps in Scenario Planning

Identify Potential Scenarios:
Begin by brainstorming potential scenarios that could impact the supply chain. Consider both internal factors (e.g., operational failures) and external factors (e.g., trade wars, pandemics). Prioritize these scenarios based on their likelihood and potential impact.

Assess the Impact:
For each scenario, evaluate the potential impact on procurement activities. This might include analyzing the financial impact, assessing supplier vulnerabilities, and determining the effect on production and delivery timelines.

Develop Response Strategies:
Create contingency plans for each high-priority scenario. These plans should outline specific actions to mitigate risk, maintain supply continuity, and minimize disruption. For example, if a key supplier faces a production shutdown, the plan might involve switching to alternative suppliers or increasing safety stock levels.

Test the Scenarios:
Conduct simulation exercises or tabletop drills to test the effectiveness of your contingency plans. This process helps identify gaps in your strategy and ensures that all stakeholders understand their roles during a disruption.

Review and Update Regularly:
Scenario planning is not a one-time exercise. Regularly review and update your scenarios and contingency plans based on new data, changing market conditions, and lessons learned from past disruptions.

Contingency Strategies for Procurement

Effective contingency strategies are the backbone of a resilient procurement strategy. They ensure that the organization can quickly adapt to unforeseen events and maintain critical operations. Key contingency strategies include:

Dual Sourcing:
For critical components, establish agreements with multiple suppliers. This dual sourcing strategy reduces the risk of disruption if one supplier fails to deliver.

Safety Stock and Buffer Inventories:
Maintaining safety stock for critical materials can cushion the impact of supply delays. The appropriate level of safety stock should be determined based on the risk profile of the supply chain and historical data.

Flexible Contracts:
Incorporate flexibility in supplier contracts to allow for adjustments during disruptions. This may include clauses for renegotiation, flexible delivery schedules, or risk-sharing provisions.

Geographical Diversification:
Source materials and components from different regions to mitigate the risk of localized disruptions. Geographical diversification spreads risk and provides alternative supply channels during regional crises.

Technology-Driven Alerts:
Use AI and machine learning tools to set up real-time alerts for potential disruptions. These technologies can monitor supplier performance, market trends, and environmental conditions to provide early warnings of potential risks.

Collaboration with Strategic Partners:
Build strategic partnerships with key suppliers to develop joint risk mitigation plans. Collaborative efforts can include sharing resources, jointly investing in risk management technologies, or co-developing contingency plans.

A Practical Example of Scenario Planning

Imagine a global consumer goods company that relies heavily on a key supplier located in a region prone to natural disasters. A scenario planning exercise might reveal that a major earthquake could disrupt production for several weeks, leading to significant delays in the supply chain. In response, the procurement team develops a contingency plan that includes:

Establishing a secondary supplier in a geographically stable region.

Increasing safety stock for critical components.

Negotiating flexible contract terms that allow for temporary price adjustments.

Setting up an AI-driven monitoring system to detect early signs of disruptions in the region.

When a minor earthquake strikes, the early warning system triggers the contingency plan. The procurement team seamlessly shifts some orders to the secondary supplier and activates increased safety stock, thereby minimizing disruption and maintaining production schedules.

Conclusion

Risk management and resilience are fundamental components of a strategic procurement function. By effectively identifying and mitigating supply chain risks, building a resilient procurement strategy, and implementing robust scenario planning and contingency strategies, organizations can safeguard against disruptions and create a more agile, responsive supply chain.

A strategic procurement manager must adopt a proactive approach to risk management, leveraging advanced technologies and data-driven insights to anticipate potential disruptions. This involves a deep understanding of various risk types—operational, financial, strategic, compliance, and environmental—and implementing tailored strategies to mitigate them. Through supplier diversification, flexible contracts, and the use of advanced analytics, procurement managers can not only reduce risks but also drive long-term value creation.

Building resilience in procurement means designing a system that is flexible, transparent, and capable of adapting to change. By integrating technology, such as AI-driven predictive analytics and blockchain for enhanced transparency, organizations can achieve real-time visibility into their supply chains. This technology-driven approach enables quick decision-making and continuous improvement, ensuring that the procurement function is always prepared for both minor disruptions and major crises.

Scenario planning and contingency strategies are essential for preparing for the unexpected. By mapping out potential scenarios and developing detailed response plans, procurement leaders ensure that their organizations are never caught off guard. Regularly testing and updating these plans keeps them relevant in a constantly evolving environment, while real-life examples demonstrate the practical benefits of a proactive approach.

Ultimately, the goal of risk management and resilience in procurement is to create a supply chain that is not only efficient and cost-effective but also robust and adaptive. This transformation enables procurement to transition from a reactive, cost-focused function to a strategic, value-driven partner in the organization. Embracing these practices provides a competitive advantage that can help companies navigate uncertainty, capitalize on opportunities, and achieve sustainable long-term growth.

As you move forward on your journey from tactical to strategic procurement management, remember that resilience is built not in moments of calm but in the preparation for and response to disruption. Invest in advanced technologies, cultivate strong supplier relationships, and embed a culture of continuous improvement. In doing so, you will create a procurement function that not only withstands the challenges of today's volatile market but also thrives and drives innovation well into the future.

This chapter has provided an in-depth exploration of risk management and resilience in procurement. By focusing on identifying and mitigating supply chain risks, building a resilient procurement strategy, and implementing scenario planning and contingency strategies, procurement leaders can secure a competitive edge and drive long-term value for their organizations.

Part 4: Navigating the Transition

From Tactical to Strategic: A Step-by-Step Guide

Transitioning from a tactical to a strategic procurement approach is not an overnight process. It requires a shift in mindset, skillset, and operational execution. Procurement professionals must move beyond simply processing transactions and instead focus on adding long-term value to the organization. This chapter provides a structured step-by-step guide to help procurement managers assess their current roles, identify skill gaps, develop a personal growth plan, and build a strategic roadmap for transformation.

Step 1: Assessing Your Current Role and Identifying Gaps

The first step in the transition process is self-assessment. To become a strategic procurement manager, you need to evaluate where you currently stand and identify areas that need improvement.

1.1 Understanding Your Current Procurement Role

Start by reviewing your daily procurement activities. Are you primarily focused on operational tasks such as processing purchase orders, negotiating prices, and managing supplier contracts? If so, you may be operating in a tactical procurement role.

A tactical procurement role typically involves:

Reactive decision-making based on immediate needs.

A focus on cost reduction rather than value creation.

Supplier selection based solely on price competitiveness.

Limited involvement in business strategy.

In contrast, a strategic procurement role includes:

Proactive decision-making based on long-term business objectives.

A focus on supplier collaboration, innovation, and risk management.

Using data analytics to drive procurement decisions.

Aligning procurement strategies with the company's overall mission and goals.

1.2 Identifying Skill and Knowledge Gaps

Once you understand your current role, the next step is to identify areas that require development. Use the following questions to guide your assessment:

Analytical Skills: Do you use data to make procurement decisions, or are decisions made based on instinct and experience?

Supplier Management: Are you building long-term relationships with suppliers, or do you frequently switch suppliers based on price?

Technology Utilization: Are you leveraging procurement software, spend analytics, and automation tools effectively?

Risk Management: Do you have a structured approach for identifying and mitigating procurement risks?

Leadership and Influence: Are you able to gain executive buy-in and collaborate effectively with other departments?

By answering these questions, you will have a clearer picture of the gaps you need to address in your journey toward strategic procurement.

Step 2: Creating a Personal Development Plan

After identifying gaps, the next step is to build a structured development plan. This plan will act as a guide to help you acquire the necessary skills and knowledge to transition into a strategic procurement role.

2.1 Enhancing Technical and Analytical Skills

To become a strategic procurement manager, you must improve your ability to analyze data and make informed decisions. Consider the following actions:

Learn Data Analytics: Take online courses on procurement analytics and spend management.

Use Technology Tools: Familiarize yourself with ERP systems, e-procurement platforms, and AI-driven procurement solutions.

Develop Financial Acumen: Understand concepts like total cost of ownership (TCO), cost-benefit analysis, and return on investment (ROI).

2.2 Strengthening Supplier Relationship Management

Strategic procurement is about building long-term, value-driven partnerships with suppliers. Enhance your supplier management skills by:

Implementing a supplier segmentation strategy to categorize vendors based on value and risk.

Collaborating with key suppliers on innovation and sustainability initiatives.

Learning advanced negotiation techniques to create win-win agreements.

2.3 Improving Leadership and Influence

Strategic procurement managers must be strong leaders who can influence stakeholders and drive organizational change. Focus

Enhancing Communication Skills: Develop the ability to articulate procurement's value to executives and stakeholders.

Building Cross-Functional Collaboration: Work closely with finance, operations, and marketing to align procurement strategies with business goals.

Gaining Executive Buy-in: Learn how to present data-driven business cases to secure leadership support for procurement initiatives.

2.4 Staying Updated on Procurement Trends

The procurement landscape is constantly evolving. Stay informed about industry trends by:

Attending procurement and supply chain conferences.

Engaging with procurement communities and professional networks.

Reading industry reports on emerging technologies, sustainable sourcing, and market shifts.

130

By continuously improving your skills and staying updated on industry trends, you will be well-positioned to make the transition to a strategic procurement role.

Step 3: Building a Roadmap for Your Transition

With a development plan in place, the final step is to create a roadmap that outlines specific actions and timelines to achieve your strategic procurement goals.

3.1 Setting Short-Term and Long-Term Goals

Define clear objectives for your transition by setting:

Short-Term Goals (3–6 months)

Learn the basics of spend analysis and procurement KPIs.

Start using procurement software to analyze historical spending data.

Engage in cross-functional collaboration with internal teams.

Mid-Term Goals (6–12 months):

Implement category management strategies.

Develop a risk management framework for procurement operations.

Establish long-term supplier partnerships and collaboration initiatives.

Long-Term Goals (1–3 years):

>Become a procurement thought leader within your organization.

>Lead strategic initiatives such as digital procurement transformation.

>Mentor junior procurement professionals on best practices.

3.2 Implementing Change Within Your Organization

Transitioning to strategic procurement also requires organizational support. Here's how to drive change within your company:

>**Educate Leadership:** Show executives how strategic procurement contributes to cost savings, efficiency, and innovation.

>**Develop a Procurement Strategy:** Align procurement activities with corporate goals to ensure strategic impact.

>**Demonstrate Quick Wins:** Implement small but impactful changes (e.g., cost-saving initiatives, supplier improvements) to build credibility.

3.3 Measuring Progress and Adjusting the Plan

Regularly review your progress and adjust your development plan as needed. Key actions include:

>**Tracking KPIs:** Measure improvements in supplier performance, cost savings, and risk reduction.

>**Seeking Feedback:** Engage with mentors, colleagues, and industry experts to refine your approach.

Celebrating Milestones: Recognize achievements along the way to stay motivated.

Conclusion

Moving from a tactical to a strategic procurement role requires dedication, learning, and proactive change management. By assessing your current role, identifying skill gaps, developing a personal growth plan, and implementing a structured roadmap, you can successfully transition into a strategic procurement leader.

This journey is not just about improving procurement processes; it's about transforming procurement into a value-adding function that drives business success. Start taking steps today, and embrace the future of procurement with confidence.

Overcoming Common Challenges

In the journey from tactical to strategic procurement, challenges are inevitable. Resistance to change, the struggle to balance day-to-day tactical responsibilities with long-term strategic initiatives, and the complexities of managing time and priorities can all hinder progress. However, by understanding these challenges and implementing targeted strategies to overcome them, procurement professionals can pave the way to becoming strategic leaders within their organizations. In this chapter, we explore these common challenges in depth and provide actionable insights to address them effectively.

Resistance to Change Within the Organization

Understanding the Roots of Resistance

Resistance to change is a natural human reaction, especially in established organizations with long-standing processes and cultural norms. In procurement, this resistance can come from various sources:

Cultural Inertia: Employees are accustomed to traditional procurement practices. Shifting from a transactional, cost-focused mindset to a strategic, value-driven approach may be met with skepticism.

Fear of the Unknown: New strategies, technologies, and processes often come with uncertainty. Stakeholders may worry about the risks of disrupting proven processes.

Perceived Loss of Control: Changes in procurement practices can be seen as a threat to established roles and responsibilities. Employees might fear that automation or new technology could render their skills obsolete.

Lack of Awareness: Resistance also stems from a lack of understanding about the benefits of the new strategic approach. Without a clear picture of how these changes drive value, employees may see them as unnecessary or disruptive.

Strategies to Overcome Resistance

Effective Communication:

Clear, transparent, and consistent communication is essential. Leaders must articulate the vision for change and explain how it aligns with the overall business strategy. Highlight the benefits—such as improved efficiency, enhanced supplier relationships, and increased value creation—and how these changes will secure long-term success. Use data, case studies, and real-world examples to support your message.

Involve Stakeholders Early:

Engage employees and stakeholders from the outset. By involving them in the planning and decision-making process, you foster a sense of ownership and reduce uncertainty. Workshops, focus groups, and regular meetings can facilitate open discussions and help address concerns before they escalate.

Education and Training:

Invest in training programs that help employees understand new technologies, methodologies, and strategic frameworks. When team members see that they are gaining valuable skills that enhance their career prospects, resistance naturally decreases. Offering certifications, workshops, and on-the-job training creates a culture of continuous learning.

Demonstrate Quick Wins:

Implement small-scale, low-risk initiatives

Case Studies and Success Stories

In the transformation journey from tactical to strategic procurement, real-world examples and success stories play a crucial role in guiding professionals through the transition. By examining how others have navigated similar challenges, procurement managers can gain valuable insights, learn best practices, and avoid common pitfalls. This chapter presents several case studies of procurement managers who successfully made the transition, highlighting their approaches, the challenges they overcame, and the lessons they learned along the way.

The Value of Learning from Experience

Every procurement organization operates in a unique environment with distinct challenges and opportunities. However, common themes emerge when organizations transition from a tactical, cost-focused approach to a strategic, value-driven function. Key themes include:

Embracing Data and Technology: Leveraging advanced analytics, ERP systems, and e_procurement tools to drive informed decision-making.

Building Strategic Supplier Relationships: Shifting from short-term, price-focused negotiations to long-term partnerships that foster innovation and risk-sharing.

Cross-Functional Collaboration: Integrating procurement strategies with broader business objectives by working closely with other departments.

Risk Management and Resilience: Implementing proactive risk management processes and developing contingency plans.

136

Leadership and Change Management: Overcoming resistance to change through strong leadership, clear communication, and continuous training.

By studying these themes in action, procurement managers can identify which strategies are most applicable to their situations and develop a roadmap for their transformation.

Case Study 1: Transforming a Global Electronics Manufacturer

Background and Challenge

A well-known global electronics manufacturer faced significant challenges with its procurement function. Historically, the company's procurement was highly transactional, focused mainly on cost-cutting without much attention to supplier relationships, innovation, or risk management. Suppliers were selected primarily on the basis of price, resulting in frequent quality issues and supply disruptions that affected production schedules. The procurement manager, recognizing that these challenges were undermining the company's competitive position, initiated a transformation project aimed at turning procurement into a strategic, value-driving function.

The Transition Journey

Assessment and Identification of Gaps:
The procurement manager began by conducting a comprehensive review of existing procurement processes, using spend analytics to identify inefficiencies. The analysis revealed several key gaps:

Over-reliance on a few low-cost suppliers leading to quality and reliability issues.

Lack of proactive risk management practices.

Insufficient use of data to drive decision-making

137

Implementing Technology and Analytics:

To address these gaps, the manager led the implementation of a new ERP system integrated with advanced spend analytics. This technology provided real-time visibility into procurement spend, supplier performance, and market trends. With data-driven insights, the procurement team could identify not only immediate cost-saving opportunities but also long-term risks and opportunities for innovation.

Strategic Sourcing and Supplier Diversification:

Using the insights from spend analysis, the manager restructured the supplier base by diversifying suppliers across multiple regions and segments. This approach reduced dependency on any single supplier and introduced a competitive dynamic that improved overall quality and reliability. Strategic sourcing practices were adopted, including long-term contracts with performance incentives that encouraged suppliers to invest in innovation and continuous improvement.

Building Cross-Functional Collaboration:

The procurement manager also established regular cross-functional meetings with teams from R&D, production, and quality assurance. These collaborative sessions helped ensure that procurement decisions were aligned with the company's strategic goals, such as reducing production downtime and driving product innovation.

Results and Lessons Learned

The transformation led to substantial improvements:

> **Quality and Reliability:** The diversified supplier base and long-term partnerships resulted in more consistent quality and fewer production disruptions.

> **Cost Savings:** While initial costs were higher due to investments in new technology and training, long-term savings were realized through improved negotiation outcomes and reduced waste.

138

Innovation: Joint innovation projects with key suppliers led to the development of new components that enhanced product performance and market competitiveness.

Lessons Learned:

Data-Driven Decision-Making: Implementing advanced analytics was crucial for identifying gaps and driving strategic decisions.

Supplier Diversification: Relying on a broader supplier base reduced risks and improved quality.

Cross-Functional Collaboration: Aligning procurement with other business functions ensured that the transformation supported overall corporate objectives.

Case Study 2: Strategic Procurement Transformation in the Automotive Industry

Background and Challenge

A leading automotive company struggled with procurement practices that were predominantly tactical. The procurement function focused on short-term cost reductions, often at the expense of long-term value creation. The result was a series of fragmented supplier relationships, frequent supply chain disruptions, and an overall inability to respond swiftly to market changes. Recognizing the need for change, the company's chief procurement officer (CPO) spearheaded a transformation initiative aimed at transitioning to a strategic procurement model.

The Transition Journey

Comprehensive Spend Analysis:
The first step was to perform a thorough spend analysis. This analysis provided a detailed view of procurement spend across different

categories and identified critical areas where cost savings were not being maximized due to inefficient practices and poor supplier performance. The analysis also highlighted the risks associated with the heavy reliance on a limited number of suppliers for key components.

Implementing Category Management:

To address these issues, the CPO introduced category management. The procurement team segmented the spend into distinct categories, allowing for tailored sourcing strategies for each category. For instance, for high-risk categories, the focus was on building long-term, collaborative relationships with suppliers, whereas for less critical categories, a competitive, price-based approach was maintained.

Establishing Strategic Supplier Relationships:

A major part of the transformation involved developing strategic relationships with key suppliers. The automotive company partnered with its suppliers on joint R&D projects, focusing on innovation in components such as electronic control units and advanced safety systems. Regular performance reviews and supplier scorecards were implemented to ensure that suppliers met the required quality and reliability standards.

Emphasizing Risk Management:

Given the inherent risks in the automotive supply chain, the CPO introduced a robust risk management framework. This framework involved continuous monitoring of supplier performance, establishing contingency plans for critical components, and creating a diversified supplier network to mitigate risks associated with supply disruptions.

Technology Integration:

Advanced procurement technologies played a pivotal role in the transformation. The company adopted a cloud-based procurement platform integrated with AI-powered analytics. This platform enabled real-time monitoring of supplier performance and market trends, providing the procurement team with the agility needed to respond to sudden disruptions or changes in market conditions.

Results and Lessons Learned

The strategic transformation yielded impressive results:

Improved Supplier Performance: The focus on long-term partnerships and regular performance monitoring led to significant improvements in supplier quality and delivery performance.

Enhanced Risk Mitigation: The diversified supplier network and robust risk management framework minimized supply chain disruptions, ensuring continuous production.

Innovation: Joint innovation initiatives with suppliers resulted in the development of cutting-edge automotive components, enhancing the company's competitive position in the market.

Cost Efficiency: Although the transition required upfront investments in technology and process redesign, the long-term savings were substantial due to improved negotiation outcomes and reduced supply chain risks.

Lessons Learned:

Importance of Category Management: Segmenting spend into distinct categories allowed for more targeted and effective sourcing strategies.

Risk Management as a Strategic Priority: Proactive risk management is essential for maintaining supply chain continuity and operational resilience.

Technology as an Enabler: Advanced procurement technologies, such as cloud-based platforms and AI analytics, provide the agility and insight needed to manage a complex supply chain.

Case Study 3: Public Sector Procurement Transformation

Background and Challenge

A regional government agency responsible for public procurement faced numerous challenges related to outdated procurement processes, siloed operations, and a lack of strategic focus. The agency's procurement function was largely administrative, focused on short-term cost savings without a clear alignment to long-term policy objectives such as sustainability, social value, and innovation. Recognizing the strategic importance of procurement in driving public value, the agency initiated a transformation project to modernize its procurement function.

The Transition Journey

Assessment and Visioning:
The transformation began with a comprehensive assessment of the agency's existing procurement processes. Stakeholder interviews, process mapping, and spend analysis revealed significant inefficiencies and missed opportunities for value creation. The agency then developed a clear vision: to transform procurement into a strategic function that supports sustainable public spending, enhances service delivery, and drives innovation in government operations.

Implementation of E_Procurement Systems:
The agency invested in an e_procurement platform that streamlined procurement processes from requisition to contract management. This system automated many routine tasks, improved transparency, and reduced administrative overhead. The platform also provided real-time analytics and reporting, which were critical for monitoring performance and ensuring compliance with new procurement policies.

Building Cross-Departmental Collaboration:
Recognizing that procurement did not operate in isolation, the agency established cross-functional teams that included representatives from finance, IT, legal, and service delivery departments. These teams worked together to redesign procurement processes, ensuring that procurement decisions were aligned with broader government priorities such as sustainability and social equity.

Developing Long-Term Supplier Partnerships:
In the public sector, building strategic supplier relationships is key to achieving long-term value. The agency restructured its supplier management approach by implementing a supplier segmentation strategy. Suppliers were categorized based on strategic importance, risk level, and their ability to deliver sustainable and ethical products or services. Long-term contracts were negotiated with key suppliers, including clauses for innovation, sustainability, and performance improvement.

Training and Capacity Building:
The transformation also involved significant investment in staff training and development. Procurement personnel received training on new e_procurement systems, data analytics, and strategic sourcing techniques. Workshops and mentoring programs were established to foster a culture of continuous learning and strategic thinking within the procurement team.

Results and Lessons Learned

The transformation of the public sector procurement function led to several noteworthy outcomes:

> **Enhanced Efficiency:** Automation and streamlined processes reduced procurement cycle times and administrative costs significantly.

> **Transparency and Accountability:** The e_procurement system improved transparency, enabling better monitoring of

spend, supplier performance, and compliance with procurement policies.

Strategic Alignment: Cross-functional collaboration ensured that procurement initiatives were aligned with government priorities, resulting in improved service delivery and greater public value.

Sustainable Procurement: By focusing on long-term supplier relationships and incorporating sustainability into procurement practices, the agency not only reduced costs but also enhanced its reputation as a responsible public entity.

Innovation in Service Delivery: Collaborative projects with key suppliers led to innovative solutions that improved public services and reduced operational risks.

Lessons Learned:

Clear Vision is Critical: Establishing a clear, strategic vision for procurement transformation helps align all stakeholders and provides direction for the entire process.

Invest in Technology and Training: Modernizing procurement systems and investing in staff development are essential for long-term success.

Foster Cross-Functional Collaboration: Breaking down silos and promoting collaboration across departments enhances the strategic impact of procurement.

Focus on Sustainability and Innovation: Integrating sustainability into procurement practices creates long-term value and drives public trust.

Best Practices and Takeaways

The case studies presented highlight several best practices that can serve as a roadmap for procurement professionals looking to make the transition from tactical to strategic roles:

Conduct a Thorough Assessment:
Before initiating any transformation, assess your current procurement processes, identify gaps, and understand the unique challenges of your supply chain. Use data analytics and stakeholder feedback to inform your strategy.

Invest in Technology:
Advanced procurement technologies—such as ERP systems, e_procurement platforms, and AI-driven analytics—are essential for driving efficiency and enabling strategic decision-making. Technology not only automates routine tasks but also provides the data needed to identify opportunities and mitigate risks.

Build Strategic Supplier Partnerships:
Develop long-term relationships with key suppliers by focusing on collaboration, trust, and joint innovation. Use flexible contracts and performance metrics to ensure continuous improvement and shared value creation.

Promote Cross-Functional Collaboration:
Engage with other departments to align procurement strategies with broader organizational goals. Regular communication and joint projects help integrate procurement into the core business strategy and foster a culture of innovation.

Emphasize Risk Management:
Develop a proactive risk management framework that includes regular risk assessments, diversified supplier strategies, and

contingency planning. Prepare for various scenarios and ensure that you have measures in place to quickly respond to disruptions.

Focus on Continuous Improvement:

Establish KPIs and performance benchmarks to monitor progress and drive continuous improvement. Regularly review your procurement strategies and processes, and be willing to adjust them based on new data and market trends.

Cultivate a Strategic Mindset:

Transitioning from a tactical to a strategic role requires a shift in mindset. Invest in leadership development, seek mentorship, and continuously expand your knowledge through professional development and industry engagement.

Conclusion

Transitioning from tactical to strategic procurement management is a transformative journey that requires deliberate planning, continuous learning, and a commitment to change. The case studies presented in this chapter illustrate that, regardless of the industry or organizational size, procurement managers who successfully make this transition share common strategies: they invest in technology, build strong supplier partnerships, foster cross-functional collaboration, and prioritize risk management and sustainability.

By assessing current processes, leveraging advanced technologies, and developing a clear strategic vision, procurement professionals can overcome the challenges of a rapidly changing business environment. The lessons learned from real-world examples demonstrate that the path to strategic procurement is not without obstacles, but those who navigate it successfully enjoy enhanced efficiency, reduced risks, and significant value creation for their organizations.

As you reflect on these success stories and best practices, consider how they can be adapted to your own context. Whether you work in the private sector, public sector, or a multinational corporation, the principles of strategic procurement remain the same: focus on long-term value, embrace innovation, and continuously strive for improvement.

The journey from tactical to strategic procurement is ongoing. It requires not only a transformation in processes and technologies but also a profound shift in mindset and culture. Embrace the challenges, learn from the successes of others, and build a robust roadmap that propels you toward a more strategic, resilient, and innovative procurement function. In doing so, you will not only drive cost savings and operational efficiencies but also position your organization for long-term success in a competitive global marketplace.

This chapter has explored real-world case studies and success stories that illustrate how procurement managers have successfully transitioned from a tactical to a strategic role. By understanding the strategies and best practices employed by these pioneers, you can apply these lessons to your own procurement journey, ensuring that you create lasting value for your organization.

Part 5: The Future of Strategic Procurement

Emerging Trends in Procurement

Shifting Business Priorities

The role of procurement has expanded far beyond securing the lowest price. Today's procurement leaders are focused on creating value, managing risk, and driving innovation. Emerging trends emphasize a more holistic approach where procurement is integrated into the broader business strategy. Organizations are increasingly recognizing procurement as a strategic partner that can influence product development, contribute to operational efficiency, and even shape corporate culture.

Key emerging trends include:

Value Creation: Modern procurement emphasizes total value rather than mere cost savings. This approach considers quality, innovation, risk mitigation, and supplier collaboration.

Data-Driven Decisions: The growing availability of big data and advanced analytics tools enables procurement teams to make informed decisions and forecast future needs with greater accuracy.

Agility and Flexibility: In an unpredictable global environment, agility is critical. Procurement strategies are evolving to become more responsive to market changes and disruptions, ensuring continuity and resilience.

Integration with Business Functions: Procurement is increasingly viewed as a cross-functional discipline. Its integration with finance, operations, R&D, and marketing enhances alignment with corporate goals.

Technology-Driven Innovation

Technology continues to drive innovation in procurement. New tools and platforms are revolutionizing how procurement functions operate, making processes more efficient and enabling deeper insights into spend, supplier performance, and market trends. Some of the technologies shaping the future include:

Artificial Intelligence (AI) and Machine Learning (ML): AI and ML are transforming procurement by enabling predictive analytics, automating routine tasks, and providing insights that help identify cost-saving opportunities. These tools can analyze historical spend data, forecast demand, and even recommend negotiation strategies.

Blockchain: Blockchain technology enhances transparency and traceability across the supply chain. It offers secure, immutable records of transactions that help verify supplier certifications, track shipments, and ensure compliance with regulatory standards.

Internet of Things (IoT): IoT devices provide real-time data on inventory levels, shipment conditions, and equipment performance. This real-time visibility is essential for proactive risk management and optimizing inventory management.

Cloud-Based Platforms: Cloud solutions enable seamless integration of procurement systems across the organization. They facilitate collaboration, real-time reporting, and scalability, allowing procurement functions to adapt quickly to changing business needs.

Robotic Process Automation (RPA): RPA automates repetitive tasks such as data entry, invoice processing, and order tracking. This frees up procurement teams to focus on strategic activities that add long-term value.

Digital Transformation and the Future of Procurement

Embracing a Digital-First Mindset

Digital transformation is not a trend; it's a fundamental shift in how organizations operate. For procurement, embracing a digital-first mindset means moving away from manual, paper-based processes to automated, integrated systems that provide real-time insights. This transformation enables procurement functions to operate more efficiently, make data-driven decisions, and ultimately drive greater value for the organization.

Digital transformation in procurement involves several key components:

Integrated Systems: Modern procurement platforms integrate with ERP systems, financial software, and supply chain management tools to create a unified view of spend, supplier performance, and inventory data. This integration improves visibility and enables better strategic planning.

Data Analytics: Advanced analytics tools turn raw data into actionable insights. Procurement teams can use these insights to identify trends, optimize supplier selection, and forecast future needs. Data-driven procurement strategies lead to more informed decisions and better negotiation outcomes.

Mobile and Cloud Technologies: Mobile applications and cloud-based systems ensure that procurement professionals have access to critical information anytime, anywhere. This flexibility is particularly important in today's fast-paced business environment, where rapid decision-making is essential.

Automation and AI: Automating routine tasks through AI-powered systems reduces the administrative burden on procurement teams, allowing them to focus on strategic initiatives. AI can also predict potential disruptions and suggest proactive measures to mitigate risks.

Benefits of Digital Transformation

The shift toward digital procurement brings numerous benefits:

Increased Efficiency: Automation and integrated systems reduce manual errors and streamline procurement processes, resulting in faster cycle times and cost savings.

Enhanced Transparency: Digital systems provide a clear audit trail, which improves accountability and facilitates regulatory compliance.

Real-Time Insights: Access to real-time data enables procurement teams to respond quickly to market changes, manage risks more effectively, and capitalize on emerging opportunities.

Improved Collaboration: Digital platforms enable seamless collaboration between procurement and other departments, ensuring that procurement strategies are aligned with broader business goals.

Scalability: Cloud-based solutions can scale with the organization's growth, ensuring that procurement processes remain robust even as operations expand.

The Role of Sustainability and ESG in Procurement

The Growing Importance of Sustainability

Sustainability has emerged as a critical consideration in procurement, driven by increasing environmental awareness, regulatory pressures, and consumer demand for ethical practices. Organizations are now held accountable not only for their financial performance but also for their impact on the environment and society. As a result, sustainable procurement practices have become essential for long-term success.

Sustainable procurement involves:

Evaluating Environmental Impact: Assessing suppliers based on their environmental performance, such as emissions, waste management, and resource efficiency.

Ensuring Social Responsibility: Ensuring that suppliers adhere to fair labor practices, support community development, and maintain ethical standards.

Integrating ESG Metrics: Incorporating ESG criteria into procurement decisions to drive improvements in sustainability and social responsibility.

Implementing Sustainable and Ethical Sourcing Practices

To integrate sustainability into procurement, organizations can adopt several strategies:

Supplier Sustainability Assessments: Evaluate potential suppliers based on their sustainability practices. Use sustainability scorecards and audits to assess environmental performance and social responsibility.

Sustainability Clauses in Contracts: Include sustainability and ethical standards in supplier contracts. This can involve requirements for environmental reporting, adherence to labor standards, and participation in sustainability initiatives.

Collaborative Innovation: Work with suppliers on joint sustainability initiatives. Collaborative projects can lead to innovations that reduce environmental impact and improve resource efficiency.

Transparency and Traceability: Implement technologies such as blockchain to ensure transparency and traceability in the supply chain. This helps verify that suppliers meet sustainability criteria and enables better monitoring of ESG performance.

Training and Awareness: Educate procurement teams on the importance of sustainability and ESG factors. Continuous training helps embed these principles into procurement practices.

Benefits of Sustainable Procurement

The adoption of sustainable procurement practices offers significant benefits:

Enhanced Brand Reputation: Organizations that prioritize sustainability build trust with consumers, investors, and other stakeholders, enhancing their brand image.

Long-Term Cost Savings: Sustainable practices often lead to improved efficiency and reduced waste, resulting in long-term cost savings.

Risk Mitigation: Sustainable procurement minimizes risks associated with regulatory non-compliance, labor disputes, and reputational damage.

Innovation and Competitiveness: Collaborating with suppliers on sustainability initiatives can drive innovation, leading to new products and processes that provide a competitive edge.

Alignment with Global Standards: Embracing ESG principles ensures that procurement practices are aligned with international standards and best practices, which is increasingly important in a globalized market.

Globalization vs. Localization in Supply Chains

The Debate: Globalization vs. Localization

The debate between globalization and localization in supply chains has gained prominence in recent years. Globalization has traditionally enabled organizations to access lower-cost suppliers and benefit from economies of scale. However, it also exposes supply chains to risks such as geopolitical tensions, longer lead times, and currency fluctuations. In contrast, localization focuses on sourcing goods and services closer to home, which can reduce risk and lead times, improve sustainability, and support local economies.

Advantages of Globalization

Globalization offers several benefits:

Cost Advantages: Access to low-cost suppliers in different regions can result in significant cost savings.

Diverse Supplier Base: A global supplier network provides access to a wider range of products and technologies, driving innovation.

Market Expansion: Global sourcing can enable organizations to tap into emerging markets and gain competitive insights from different regions.

155

However, global supply chains are also vulnerable to disruptions such as trade disputes, natural disasters, and political instability. These factors can lead to delays, increased costs, and reduced flexibility.

Advantages of Localization

Localization in procurement focuses on sourcing from local or regional suppliers. This approach offers distinct benefits:

Reduced Lead Times: Proximity to suppliers generally leads to faster delivery times, improving responsiveness.

Enhanced Flexibility: Local suppliers can often adapt more quickly to changes in demand or market conditions.

Sustainability Benefits: Local sourcing reduces transportation emissions and supports local economies, aligning with sustainability goals.

Risk Mitigation: By reducing reliance on global supply chains, organizations can better manage risks associated with international disruptions.

Localization, however, may come with higher costs compared to global sourcing, and the range of available suppliers might be more limited.

Balancing Global and Local Strategies

The future of procurement likely lies in striking the right balance between globalization and localization. A hybrid approach allows organizations to enjoy the benefits of both models while mitigating their respective risks. Key considerations for balancing global and local sourcing include:

Risk Assessment: Evaluate the risk profiles of global suppliers versus local alternatives. For critical or high-risk items, localization may provide greater security.

Cost-Benefit Analysis: Conduct a thorough cost-benefit analysis that considers not just the purchase price but also the total cost of ownership, including transportation, tariffs, and potential disruption costs.

Supply Chain Flexibility: Develop flexible procurement strategies that allow for rapid switching between global and local suppliers based on current market conditions.

Sustainability Goals: Align sourcing decisions with sustainability objectives. Local sourcing may support lower emissions and community development, while global sourcing can offer access to advanced technologies and innovations.

Strategic Partnerships: Build strategic partnerships with both global and local suppliers. This diversified supplier base can enhance resilience and provide the best of both worlds in terms of cost, quality, and responsiveness.

Case Example: A Hybrid Approach

Consider a consumer electronics company that historically relied on global suppliers to source components. While this approach provided cost advantages, the company experienced delays and quality issues during geopolitical tensions and natural disasters. In response, the procurement team adopted a hybrid strategy:

Global Sourcing for Standard Components: The company continued to source non-critical components globally to take advantage of cost efficiencies.

Local Sourcing for Critical Components: For critical components that directly impacted product quality and production timelines, the company shifted to local suppliers. This change reduced lead times and improved responsiveness.

Dual Sourcing: In some cases, the company implemented dual sourcing—using both global and local suppliers for the same component—to ensure a backup in case of disruptions.

This hybrid strategy not only enhanced supply chain resilience but also improved overall product quality and customer satisfaction, demonstrating that balancing globalization with localization can be a winning approach.

Conclusion

The future of strategic procurement is shaped by the interplay of emerging trends, digital transformation, sustainability imperatives, and the evolving dynamics of global and local supply chains. As organizations navigate an increasingly complex and volatile marketplace, procurement functions must evolve to become strategic drivers of value.

Digital transformation is revolutionizing procurement by integrating advanced technologies such as AI, machine learning, blockchain, and IoT. These tools enhance efficiency, provide real-time insights, and enable proactive decision-making. By leveraging these technologies, procurement teams can optimize spend, improve supplier performance, and mitigate risks more effectively.

Sustainability and ESG have emerged as non-negotiable elements of modern procurement. Organizations are expected to not only deliver cost savings but also to contribute positively to the environment and society. Sustainable and ethical sourcing practices ensure that procurement decisions align with global standards and stakeholder expectations, enhancing corporate reputation and driving long-term value.

The ongoing debate between globalization and localization in supply chains highlights the need for a balanced approach. While global sourcing offers cost advantages and access to a diverse supplier base, localization can reduce lead times, enhance flexibility, and support sustainability goals. A hybrid approach that combines the best of both worlds can provide a resilient and agile supply chain capable of adapting to disruptions and evolving market conditions.

In summary, the future of strategic procurement lies in embracing innovation, integrating advanced technologies, and aligning procurement practices with broader organizational goals. As you look ahead, focus on developing a digital-first mindset, building sustainable supplier partnerships, and balancing global and local sourcing strategies. These elements are critical for creating a procurement function that is not only efficient and cost-effective but also resilient, innovative, and capable of driving long-term growth.

The transformation from tactical to strategic procurement is an ongoing journey. By staying informed about emerging trends, investing in digital technologies, prioritizing sustainability, and carefully balancing sourcing strategies, procurement leaders can position their functions as indispensable strategic partners. The road ahead is filled with opportunities—seize them to build a future-ready procurement function that delivers sustainable value and competitive advantage.

Embrace the future of procurement with a strategic vision, continuous innovation, and a commitment to excellence. The integration of digital tools, sustainability practices, and a balanced approach to global and local sourcing will not only enhance your procurement operations but also contribute significantly to your organization's overall success in a rapidly evolving business landscape.

Becoming a Thought Leader in Procurement

In today's competitive business landscape, procurement is evolving from a back-office function into a strategic powerhouse. As organizations increasingly rely on procurement to drive value creation, cost savings, and innovation, establishing yourself as a thought leader in procurement becomes not only a personal career milestone but also a means to influence the industry at large. This chapter explores how to build your personal brand as a strategic procurement expert, harness networking and professional development opportunities, and actively contribute to the procurement community. By embracing these practices, you can elevate your role, drive change, and leave a lasting impact on the procurement field.

Building Your Personal Brand as a Strategic Procurement Expert

Define Your Unique Value Proposition

The first step in becoming a thought leader is to identify what makes you unique. Ask yourself:

What expertise or experiences do you bring to the table?

What are your core strengths in strategic sourcing, supplier relationship management, risk mitigation, or procurement technology?

How have you transformed procurement functions in your past roles?

Your unique value proposition should be clear and compelling. It's the promise of value you offer to your organization and to the broader procurement community. Whether you have a knack for leveraging digital transformation, driving sustainability initiatives, or implementing innovative risk management strategies, articulate that clearly in your personal narrative.

Develop a Consistent Messaging Platform

Once you've defined your value proposition, develop a consistent messaging platform that reflects your professional identity. This platform should be evident across all your professional touchpoints—your resume, LinkedIn profile, professional blog, and even your speaking engagements. Key elements include:

> **Professional Biography:** Craft a biography that outlines your journey from tactical to strategic procurement, emphasizing key achievements and learnings.

> **Thought Leadership Content:** Regularly produce content that reflects your expertise. This can include articles, white papers, case studies, or even social media posts that discuss industry trends, best practices, or innovative approaches in procurement.

> **Visual Identity:** Consistency in visuals—such as a professional headshot, branded slides for presentations, and a cohesive color scheme—reinforces your personal brand and makes you easily recognizable.

Showcase Your Expertise

Establishing credibility is crucial. Consider the following actions to showcase your expertise:

Publish Articles and Blogs: Write in-depth articles that address complex procurement challenges, innovative solutions, and strategic insights. These publications can be shared on your blog, LinkedIn, or industry-specific platforms.

Speak at Conferences and Webinars: Participating as a speaker at industry conferences and webinars positions you as an expert. Discuss topics such as digital transformation in procurement, sustainable sourcing, or effective supplier collaboration.

Engage in Social Media: Platforms like LinkedIn and Twitter are excellent venues to share your insights, comment on industry news, and engage with other thought leaders. Consistent, insightful contributions build your reputation over time.

Collaborate with Industry Publications: Partner with established procurement publications to contribute guest posts or expert opinions. This exposure can significantly boost your credibility and visibility.

Networking and Professional Development Opportunities

The Power of Networking

Networking is a cornerstone for thought leadership. By building a strong professional network, you not only gain access to new ideas and trends but also create opportunities for collaboration and career advancement. Networking should be viewed as a two-way street—while you share your knowledge and insights, you also learn from peers and industry veterans.

Strategies for Effective Networking

Attend Industry Conferences and Events:
Conferences, trade shows, and industry events provide

opportunities to meet peers, potential mentors, and industry influencers. Engage actively by participating in panel discussions, workshops, and networking sessions.

Join Professional Associations:
Organizations such as the Chartered Institute of Procurement & Supply (CIPS), Institute for Supply Management (ISM), and various regional procurement groups offer access to exclusive events, training, and forums. Membership in these associations not only provides networking opportunities but also access to cutting-edge research and best practices.

Engage on Social Media:
LinkedIn groups, Twitter chats, and other online communities focused on procurement are excellent for exchanging ideas, sharing articles, and discussing challenges. Be proactive—ask questions, share your experiences, and connect with others who share your passion for procurement innovation.

Participate in Webinars and Virtual Workshops:
With the rise of digital events, webinars have become a vital part of professional development. They offer convenient access to industry experts and provide valuable insights into emerging trends and technologies.

Build Relationships with Mentors:
Identify leaders in procurement who inspire you and reach out to them for mentorship. A mentor can provide guidance, feedback, and help accelerate your growth. Don't hesitate to ask for advice on navigating the complexities of transitioning to a strategic role.

Professional Development

Continuous learning is essential in an industry as dynamic as procurement. Investing in professional development not only hones your skills but also demonstrates your commitment to the field. Here are some avenues for professional growth:

Certifications and Courses:

Earning certifications such as the Certified Professional in Supply Management (CPSM), Certified Supply Chain Professional (CSCP), or those offered by CIPS can significantly enhance your knowledge and credibility. Additionally, online courses on data analytics, digital procurement, and risk management can keep you updated on emerging trends.

Workshops and Seminars:

Participating in workshops and seminars offers hands-on learning opportunities. These events often focus on practical applications of new technologies, innovative sourcing strategies, or advanced negotiation technique

Industry Publications and Research:

Stay current with the latest research by subscribing to industry journals, blogs, and newsletters. Reading white papers, case studies, and market reports can provide fresh perspectives and insights that you can apply in your role.

Academic Programs:

Consider enrolling in advanced degree programs or executive education courses in supply chain management, procurement strategy, or business analytics. Many universities now offer specialized programs that blend theoretical knowledge with practical application.

Internal Training Programs:

Leverage your organization's internal training resources. Many companies offer leadership development programs, mentorship opportunities, and cross-functional training that can help you build a more strategic perspective.

Networking with Peers:
Peer-to-peer learning is invaluable. Joining study groups, attending local meetups, or even organizing informal discussions with colleagues can expose you to new ideas and collaborative problem-solving approaches.

The Role of Continuous Improvement

A key component of professional development is the commitment to continuous improvement. This means not only acquiring new skills but also consistently refining existing processes. A mindset of continuous improvement encourages you to regularly assess your performance, seek feedback, and make adjustments as needed. Use performance metrics and KPIs to track your progress and set new targets for growth.

Contributing to the Procurement Community

Sharing Knowledge and Best Practices

Becoming a thought leader means giving back to the community. Contributing your insights and experiences helps shape the future of procurement and establishes you as an authority in the field.

How to Contribute

Write Articles and White Papers:
Document your experiences and insights by writing articles or white papers on procurement topics. Whether you're discussing a successful strategic initiative or sharing lessons learned from a challenging project, your insights can help peers navigate similar challenges.

Participate in Industry Forums:
Join and contribute to online forums, discussion groups, and social media communities. Platforms like LinkedIn,

industry-specific websites, and professional associations offer opportunities to share knowledge and engage with peers.

Speak at Conferences and Webinars:
Public speaking is a powerful way to disseminate your ideas. Whether you present at conferences, lead webinars, or participate in panel discussions, sharing your experiences in person or virtually can amplify your influence.

Mentorship Programs:
Offer your expertise to mentor emerging procurement professionals. Mentorship not only helps others grow but also reinforces your own understanding and positions you as a leader in the field.

Develop and Share Tools:
If you've developed effective frameworks, templates, or tools that have helped improve procurement processes in your organization, consider sharing them with the wider community. This could be through blog posts, webinars, or collaborative platforms.

Join Professional Associations:
Active participation in organizations like CIPS or ISM not only offers networking opportunities but also provides platforms to contribute to industry standards and best practices. Serving on committees or working groups further enhances your visibility and influence.

The Benefits of Contributing

Contributing to the procurement community offers several benefits:

Enhanced Credibility: Sharing your knowledge builds your reputation as an expert and can lead to more speaking engagements, consulting opportunities, and career advancements.

Networking Opportunities: Engaging with other professionals expands your network, which can open doors to collaborations, partnerships, and new business opportunities.

Continuous Learning: Interacting with peers and participating in industry discussions exposes you to new ideas and challenges your thinking, fostering continuous improvement.

Influence on the Industry: By contributing to the community, you help shape the future of procurement practices and standards. Your insights can influence how organizations approach strategic procurement on a global scale.

Case Study: Building a Thought Leadership Brand

Consider the case of a senior procurement manager at a multinational consumer goods company. Recognizing the need for strategic innovation, this leader began documenting successful initiatives that transformed the company's procurement processes. They started by writing detailed case studies about their strategic sourcing projects, which were published in industry journals and on professional blogs. Over time, they began speaking at conferences and hosting webinars focused on topics such as leveraging data analytics in procurement and building sustainable supplier partnerships.

Through consistent content creation and public speaking, the manager built a robust personal brand. Their insights were widely shared, leading to invitations to contribute to leading procurement publications and to participate in industry roundtables. This thought leadership not only advanced their career but also helped their organization by positioning it as an industry leader in strategic procurement.

Lessons Learned:

Consistency is Key: Regular contributions, whether through articles, talks, or online posts, build your reputation over time.

Engage Authentically: Authentic engagement with the community fosters trust and creates opportunities for meaningful connections.

Leverage Multiple Channels: Utilize various platforms—blogs, social media, webinars, and conferences—to reach a wider audience.

Showcase Impact: Use data, case studies, and testimonials to demonstrate the real-world impact of your procurement initiatives.

Conclusion

Becoming a thought leader in procurement is a transformative journey that extends far beyond personal career advancement. It involves building a robust personal brand, actively engaging in professional development and networking, and contributing meaningfully to the broader procurement community. By positioning yourself as an expert, you not only enhance your own career prospects but also drive industry innovation, shape best practices, and create lasting value for your organization.

Your journey to thought leadership begins with a clear understanding of your unique value proposition and a commitment to continuous learning. Invest in your personal development, embrace opportunities for networking, and share your insights openly. Whether through writing articles, speaking at events, mentoring colleagues, or contributing to industry forums, every step you take will amplify your influence and solidify your position as a strategic procurement leader.

As the procurement landscape continues to evolve—driven by digital transformation, sustainability imperatives, and global market dynamics—the need for thought leaders who can navigate these changes and inspire innovation will only grow. Embrace the challenge, invest in your growth, and actively contribute to the community. In doing so, you not only build a powerful personal brand but also help shape the future of strategic procurement.

In summary, the road to thought leadership in procurement is paved with continuous learning, proactive engagement, and a passion for driving change. By building your personal brand, leveraging professional development opportunities, and contributing to the procurement community, you can position yourself as an influential voice in the field. This not only enhances your own career but also ensures that procurement evolves from a supportive function into a critical, strategic driver of organizational success.

Embrace the journey, share your expertise, and become a beacon of innovation in the world of procurement. The future of procurement is bright, and as a thought leader, you have the power to shape it for the better.

This chapter has detailed how to become a thought leader in procurement by building a strong personal brand, actively networking, and contributing to the procurement community. By sharing your expertise and engaging with peers, you not only elevate your own career but also drive strategic innovation and best practices in procurement management.

Conclusion: Your Journey to Strategic Procurement

The transformation from tactical to strategic procurement is not just a professional evolution—it's a fundamental shift that redefines how you, as a procurement leader, contribute to your organization's success. As we conclude this book, it's time to reflect on the journey, recap key takeaways, and chart a course for the future. This final chapter is an invitation to embrace change, take that first bold step, and commit to a long-term vision that will not only redefine your career but also create lasting value for your organization.

Recap of Key Takeaways

1. The Strategic Procurement Mindset

The transition to strategic procurement starts with a change in mindset. Rather than focusing solely on day-to-day transactions and cost reduction, strategic procurement emphasizes long-term value creation, supplier collaboration, and risk management. This shift requires you to:

> **Embrace Data and Technology:** Use advanced analytics, ERP systems, and e_procurement platforms to drive informed decisions.

> **Cultivate Innovation:** Look beyond immediate cost savings by seeking out opportunities for innovation throughout the supply chain.

> **Prioritize Risk Management:** Build resilient strategies that protect your organization against disruptions and uncertainties.

Foster Collaboration: Transform supplier relationships into strategic partnerships that drive joint value creation and continuous improvement.

2. Core Competencies and Skills

Throughout the book, we explored the core competencies required to excel in strategic procurement. These include:

Analytical Thinking: Leveraging data-driven insights to inform decisions and optimize procurement processes.

Negotiation and Relationship Management: Building lasting, mutually beneficial relationships with suppliers while securing favorable terms.

Financial Acumen and TCO Analysis: Understanding the total cost of ownership and its impact on long-term financial performance.

Risk Management and Resilience: Identifying, assessing, and mitigating risks to ensure supply chain continuity.

Leadership and Influence: Leading cross-functional teams, influencing stakeholders, and driving organizational change.

3. Implementing Strategic Procurement Practices

Implementing strategic procurement practices is the foundation upon which you build a future-ready procurement function. Key practices include:

Strategic Sourcing: Developing sourcing strategies that align with corporate goals, using data analytics to identify and negotiate with the best suppliers.

Category Management and Segmentation: Organizing spend into distinct categories to tailor strategies for cost savings, risk reduction, and value creation.

Supplier Relationship Management (SRM): Transitioning from transactional vendor interactions to long-term partnerships that foster innovation and resilience.

Sustainable and Ethical Sourcing: Integrating ESG (Environmental, Social, Governance) considerations to build a responsible and sustainable supply chain.

4. Driving Innovation Through Procurement

Innovation is a critical driver of long-term success in procurement. The ability to identify innovation opportunities in the supply chain, collaborate with suppliers, and leverage market trends is essential for:

Co-Creating Value: Working hand-in-hand with suppliers to develop new products, processes, and strategies.

Capitalizing on Market Disruptions: Turning challenges into opportunities through proactive risk management and agile responses to change.

Embedding a Culture of Innovation: Encouraging continuous improvement and forward-thinking approaches within your procurement team.

5. Navigating the Transition and Overcoming Challenges

The journey from tactical to strategic procurement is filled with challenges—resistance to change, balancing tactical responsibilities with strategic initiatives, and managing time and priorities effectively. Key strategies to overcome these obstacles include:

Self-Assessment: Regularly evaluate your current role and identify areas for growth.

Personal Development: Create a comprehensive development plan, including training, mentorship, and professional certifications.

Change Management: Engage stakeholders, build cross-functional teams, and demonstrate quick wins to build momentum.

Time Management: Prioritize tasks, delegate effectively, and use technology to streamline operations.

Encouragement to Take the First Step

Change can be daunting, but the journey from tactical to strategic procurement is one of empowerment and growth. It's not enough to simply understand the theory—you must put it into practice. The first step is often the hardest, but it's also the most critical.

Start by assessing your current procurement practices and identifying areas where you can introduce strategic changes. Whether it's integrating a new technology tool, renegotiating supplier contracts with a focus on long-term value, or simply initiating a conversation about risk management with your team, every small step contributes to your overall transformation.

Remember, the journey of a thousand miles begins with a single step. As you take that step, lean on the tools, frameworks, and strategies discussed throughout this book. Use data to drive your decisions, embrace innovative approaches, and continuously seek opportunities for improvement.

The Long-Term Impact of Becoming a Strategic Procurement Manager

Transforming Organizational Value

Transitioning to a strategic procurement role doesn't just impact your day-to-day work—it transforms the entire organization. Strategic procurement creates significant long-term benefits, including:

Cost Efficiency and Savings: By focusing on total cost of ownership and strategic sourcing, you can secure sustainable cost savings that boost the organization's profitability.

Enhanced Supplier Performance: Long-term, collaborative supplier relationships lead to better quality, innovation, and reliability, reducing operational risks.

Agility and Resilience: A proactive approach to risk management and continuous improvement builds a resilient supply chain that can adapt to disruptions and market changes.

Competitive Advantage: Organizations that embrace strategic procurement are better positioned to innovate, enter new markets, and respond quickly to evolving customer demands.

Professional Growth and Leadership

Becoming a strategic procurement manager also accelerates your professional development. As you cultivate advanced skills and adopt a forward-thinking mindset, you position yourself as an indispensable leader within your organization. This transition opens doors to higher-level roles, such as procurement director or chief procurement officer, and provides opportunities for greater influence over organizational strategy.

Moreover, the journey to strategic procurement is a journey of continuous learning and improvement. Every challenge you overcome and every innovation you implement adds to your experience and credibility, paving the way for a successful career built on strategic thinking and leadership.

Impact on the Industry

By transforming your approach to procurement, you not only drive success within your organization but also contribute to the broader procurement community. As more professionals embrace strategic procurement, best practices evolve, industry standards improve, and the role of procurement as a strategic function becomes widely recognized. Your contributions—whether through thought leadership, mentorship, or sharing success stories—help shape the future of the field and inspire others to follow in your footsteps.

Call to Action: Start Implementing the Strategies Today

The journey from tactical to strategic procurement is an exciting, transformative process that has the power to redefine not only your career but also the success of your organization. The strategies, tools, and best practices discussed in this book are not theoretical—they are actionable steps that you can start implementing today.

Take Action Now

Assess Your Current State:
Begin by conducting a self-assessment of your procurement practices. Identify what is working well and where improvements can be made. Use this insight to develop a clear roadmap for your transition.

Invest in Your Development:
Commit to continuous learning through professional certifications, advanced training courses, and industry events. Expand your skill set in areas such as data analytics, risk management, and strategic sourcing. Remember, every new skill

you acquire brings you closer to your goal of becoming a strategic procurement leader.

Embrace Technology:
Evaluate your current procurement tools and consider integrating advanced digital solutions such as AI-driven analytics, cloud-based ERP systems, and e_procurement platforms. Leverage these technologies to enhance efficiency, improve decision-making, and drive long-term value.

Build Strong Relationships:
Foster collaborative relationships both within your organization and with external suppliers. Engage with other departments to ensure that procurement strategies are aligned with broader business objectives. Develop long-term supplier partnerships that prioritize innovation and risk-sharing.

Develop a Strategic Roadmap:
Create a detailed, actionable roadmap that outlines your short-term, mid-term, and long-term goals for transitioning to strategic procurement. This roadmap should include specific initiatives, milestones, and KPIs to track your progress. Regularly review and adjust your plan based on feedback and changing market conditions.

Engage with the Community:
Join procurement forums, professional associations, and online communities to connect with like-minded professionals. Share your experiences, learn from others, and contribute to the evolution of best practices in the field. Your engagement not only enhances your personal growth but also strengthens the entire procurement community.

The Future Awaits

Becoming a strategic procurement manager is not a destination—it's an ongoing journey. Every step you take, no matter how small, contributes to a broader transformation that drives innovation, efficiency, and sustainable success. By embracing the strategies outlined in this book, you are positioning yourself at the forefront of procurement evolution, ready to lead your organization through the complexities of a dynamic global marketplace.

Your journey to strategic procurement is a testament to your commitment to excellence, continuous improvement, and leadership. It is an opportunity to redefine your role, influence change, and create lasting value for your organization. As you embark on this journey, remember that the future of procurement is bright, and the skills and insights you develop today will shape the industry for years to come.

Final Thoughts

The journey from tactical to strategic procurement management is challenging, rewarding, and transformative. It requires a deliberate shift in mindset, an investment in your professional development, and a commitment to continuous improvement. In this book, we have covered everything from the core competencies needed for strategic procurement to the practical steps required for transformation. We've explored how to leverage technology, build supplier relationships, manage risks, and drive innovation.

Now, as you stand at the threshold of this transformation, know that the power to create lasting impact lies in your hands. Embrace the change, take the first step, and join the growing community of strategic procurement professionals who are redefining what it means to be a procurement leader.

Your future as a strategic procurement manager is not just about achieving cost savings—it's about driving long-term value, fostering innovation, and contributing to your organization's overall success. Every initiative you implement, every supplier relationship you build, and every strategic decision you make brings you closer to this goal.

The world of procurement is evolving, and the strategic leader is at its helm. Now is the time to step up, harness the power of strategic procurement, and lead your organization to new heights. Start implementing these strategies today, share your journey with your peers, and become an influential voice in the procurement community.

Join the community of strategic procurement professionals who are committed to transforming their organizations and shaping the future of the industry. Your journey to strategic procurement begins with one bold step—take that step now and pave the way for a future where procurement is recognized as a cornerstone of business success.

Embrace the challenge, invest in your growth, and let your journey inspire others. The future of procurement is in your hands—make it a future defined by innovation, resilience, and strategic excellence.

This chapter has recapped the essential takeaways from your journey, provided actionable steps to begin the transition, and outlined the long-term benefits of evolving into a strategic procurement manager. With determination, continuous learning, and a strategic mindset, you can overcome any challenge and drive meaningful change within your organization. Now is the time to take action and embark on your journey to strategic procurement management.

Appendices

The appendices in this book are designed to serve as a comprehensive resource for procurement professionals who are on the journey from tactical to strategic procurement management. Whether you are looking to enhance your skills, streamline your processes, or simply get a quick refresher on key terms, these appendices provide valuable tools, templates, and definitions to support your growth and success.

This chapter is divided into three main sections:

Appendix A: Tools and Resources for Procurement Professionals
Recommended books, courses, certifications, and a list of procurement software and platforms.

Appendix B: Templates and Frameworks
Practical resources including strategic sourcing templates, supplier evaluation scorecards, and risk assessment frameworks.

Appendix C: Glossary of Procurement Terms
A quick-reference guide to key terms and definitions that are essential in procurement.

Each section is intended to be a living resource—something you can return to as you develop your procurement strategy and enhance your skills over time.

Appendix A: Tools and Resources for Procurement Professionals

Recommended Books

Reading is a cornerstone of professional development. The following books are highly recommended for procurement professionals aiming to deepen their strategic understanding and refine their skills:

"The Purchasing Chessboard" by Christian Schuh et al.
This book offers 64 methods to reduce cost and increase value with suppliers. It provides practical strategies and frameworks for strategic sourcing and category management.

"Vested: How P&G, McDonald's, and Microsoft are Redefining Winning in Business Relationships" by Kate Vitasek and Karl Manrodt.
Learn how innovative companies are transforming procurement relationships from transactional to collaborative partnerships that drive long-term value.

"Procurement 4.0: A Survival Guide in a Digital World" by Bernardo Nicoletti.
An insightful guide to integrating digital technologies into procurement practices, helping you navigate the digital transformation journey.

"Category Management in Purchasing" by Jonathan O'Brien.
This book provides an in-depth look at category management techniques and best practices, helping you segment your spend and tailor strategies for each category.

"Strategic Procurement Management: Concepts and Cases" by Jeanne M. Kenny.
A comprehensive resource that combines theoretical insights with real-world case studies, offering a clear roadmap for transforming procurement functions.

Recommended Courses and Certifications

Continuous education is key to staying ahead in a rapidly evolving procurement landscape. Here are some courses and certifications that can boost your career:

Certified Professional in Supply Management (CPSM):
Offered by the Institute for Supply Management (ISM), this certification covers strategic sourcing, supplier relationship management, and risk management. It is widely recognized as a standard for procurement excellence.

Certified Supply Chain Professional (CSCP):
Provided by APICS, this certification is ideal for those looking to broaden their knowledge of the end-to-end supply chain and integrate procurement strategy with overall supply chain management.

Chartered Institute of Procurement & Supply (CIPS) Courses:
CIPS offers a range of courses—from foundational to advanced—that cover topics such as strategic sourcing, contract management, and sustainable procurement practices.

Procurement and Supply Management Certificate Programs:
Many universities and online platforms (such as Coursera, edX, and LinkedIn Learning) offer certificate programs in procurement and supply chain management. These programs are designed to enhance both technical skills and strategic thinking.

Workshops and Webinars:
Regularly participate in industry workshops and webinars. These events offer practical insights on emerging trends, digital transformation, and best practices in procurement.

Procurement Software and Platforms

Leveraging the right technology is crucial for transitioning from tactical to strategic procurement. Here's a list of some popular procurement software and platforms that can help you streamline operations, analyze data, and manage supplier relationships:

SAP Ariba:
A comprehensive platform that covers sourcing, procurement, contract management, and supplier collaboration. It integrates with ERP systems to provide real-time insights and analytics.

Coupa:
Known for its spend management capabilities, Coupa offers an easy-to-use interface that helps organizations manage procurement processes, track spend, and optimize supplier relationships.

Jaggaer:
A cloud-based procurement solution that provides tools for strategic sourcing, supplier management, and spend analytics. Jaggaer is widely used across industries for its scalability and robust features.

Oracle Procurement Cloud:
A powerful solution for automating procurement processes, Oracle's platform offers features such as e_procurement, supplier management, and real-time reporting, enabling a digital transformation in procurement.

GEP SMART:
A unified procurement platform that integrates sourcing, procurement, and contract management. It provides advanced analytics and reporting features to help drive strategic decisions.

Ivalua:
This platform is designed for end-to-end procurement management, offering tools for sourcing, supplier management, and spend analysis. Ivalua's flexible architecture makes it a popular choice among global organizations.

Zycus:
Zycus offers a suite of procurement solutions, including spend analysis, strategic sourcing, and contract management. Its AI-powered tools help organizations automate and optimize procurement processes.

These tools not only enhance operational efficiency but also provide the data and insights necessary for strategic decision-making, enabling you to drive long-term value and innovation.

Appendix B: Templates and Frameworks

Templates and frameworks serve as practical tools that help streamline procurement processes and ensure consistency. This appendix provides a range of templates and frameworks that you can adapt to your organization's needs.

Strategic Sourcing Templates

A strategic sourcing template is designed to guide the entire sourcing process—from initial analysis to supplier selection and negotiation. Here's an outline of key elements to include in your strategic sourcing template:

Spend Analysis:

Historical spend data

Key cost drivers

Opportunities for consolidation

Market Research:

Supplier landscape overview

Market trends and forecasts

Competitive analysis

Supplier Evaluation Criteria:

Cost competitiveness

Quality standards

Delivery performance

Innovation capability

Risk factors

Sourcing Strategy Development:

Objectives and goals

Risk assessment and mitigation strategies

Long-term value creation plans

Negotiation and Contracting:

Desired contract terms

Performance metrics

Contingency plans

Evaluation of potential risks and opportunities

Implementation and Monitoring:

Action plan with timelines

Key performance indicators (KPIs)

Continuous improvement measures

This template can be customized based on specific procurement categories and organizational requirements, ensuring that every strategic sourcing initiative is aligned with your overall business strategy.

Supplier Evaluation Scorecards

Supplier evaluation is a critical component of strategic procurement. A supplier evaluation scorecard provides a structured method to assess supplier performance and make data-driven decisions. Here's a sample structure for a supplier evaluation scorecard:

Quality:

Product or service quality rating

Defect rates

Compliance with quality standards

Cost:

Price competitiveness

Total cost of ownership (TCO)

Payment terms and conditions

Delivery:

On-time delivery rate

Lead times

Flexibility in meeting changing demands

Innovation:

Capability to introduce new technologies or processes

Collaborative initiatives for product or process improvement

Risk Management:

Financial stability

Risk mitigation strategies

Supplier's contingency plans

Sustainability and Ethics:

Adherence to environmental and social standards

Ethical sourcing practices

Commitment to sustainability initiatives

Overall Relationship:

Communication effectiveness

Responsiveness to issues

Long-term partnership potential

Each criterion can be assigned a weight based on its importance to your organization. Regularly updating and reviewing the scorecard ensures that supplier performance is monitored consistently and that high-performing suppliers are recognized and nurtured.

Risk Assessment Frameworks

A robust risk assessment framework is essential for identifying and mitigating risks in procurement. This framework should be designed to evaluate risks across multiple dimensions and provide a clear action plan for risk mitigation. Key components of a risk assessment framework include:

Risk Identification:

List potential risks (e.g., operational, financial, strategic, compliance, environmental)

Categorize risks based on their source and impact

Risk Analysis:

Assess the likelihood of each risk occurring

Evaluate the potential impact on the organization

Prioritize risks based on a combination of likelihood and impact

Risk Mitigation Strategies:

Develop contingency plans for high-priority risks

Implement risk mitigation measures (e.g., supplier diversification, safety stock, flexible contracts)

Define roles and responsibilities for managing each risk

Monitoring and Reporting:

Establish key risk indicators (KRIs

Set up a risk dashboard for real-time monitoring

Schedule regular risk review meetings to update the risk register

Continuous Improvement:

Collect feedback from stakeholders

Adjust risk strategies based on new data and market conditions

Document lessons learned and best practices for future reference

Using this framework, procurement professionals can systematically assess risks and implement targeted strategies to ensure supply chain resilience and operational continuity.

Appendix C: Glossary of Procurement Terms

A well-defined glossary is a valuable resource for both seasoned procurement professionals and those new to the field. It provides quick reference definitions of key terms, ensuring that everyone is on the same page when discussing procurement strategies and processes. Below is a glossary of essential procurement terms:

Advance Procurement:
The process of planning and purchasing goods or services well ahead of when they are needed, often to secure better pricing or guarantee availability.

Category Management:
A strategic approach that organizes procurement spend into

discrete groups based on similar characteristics, enabling tailored sourcing strategies for each category.

Digital Transformation:
The integration of digital technology into all aspects of procurement processes, leading to significant changes in how organizations operate and deliver value.

E-Procurement:
The use of digital platforms to automate procurement processes, from requisition and order processing to contract management and supplier collaboration.

Enterprise Resource Planning (ERP):
An integrated software system used to manage and automate core business processes, including procurement, finance, supply chain, and human resources.

Key Performance Indicators (KPIs):
Quantitative metrics used to evaluate the performance of procurement processes, such as cost savings, supplier performance, and cycle times.

Lean Procurement:
An approach that focuses on eliminating waste and inefficiencies in the procurement process to reduce costs and improve overall performance.

Risk Management:
The process of identifying, assessing, and mitigating risks that could impact procurement and supply chain operations.

Scenario Planning:
A strategic planning method that considers various future scenarios and develops contingency plans to address potential disruptions.

Strategic Sourcing:
A holistic approach to procurement that focuses on long-term value creation rather than short-term cost reduction, involving supplier evaluation, market research, and contract negotiation.

Supplier Relationship Management (SRM):
A systematic approach to managing interactions with suppliers to maximize the value of supplier relationships, enhance collaboration, and drive continuous improvement.

Sustainability in Procurement:
The practice of sourcing goods and services in a way that minimizes environmental impact, supports social responsibility, and ensures long-term resource availability.

Total Cost of Ownership (TCO):
A comprehensive measure that considers all costs associated with the acquisition, operation, maintenance, and disposal of a product or service over its entire lifecycle.

Value Creation:
The process of generating additional value—beyond cost savings—through strategic procurement practices that drive innovation, quality, and long-term competitive advantage.

Final Thoughts

These appendices are designed to be your go-to reference as you advance on your journey from tactical to strategic procurement. They provide the tools, templates, and terminology needed to not only implement best practices but also to continually improve and innovate within your procurement function.

By leveraging the recommended books, courses, certifications, and software platforms, you can deepen your expertise and stay current with industry trends. The templates and frameworks provided are practical tools to help you standardize your processes, evaluate supplier performance, and manage risk effectively. And the glossary ensures that you have a common language for discussing procurement strategies and innovations.

As you move forward, remember that continuous improvement is key. Use these appendices as a living resource—update them as new tools emerge, new best practices are identified, and new trends shape the industry. Your journey to strategic procurement management is ongoing, and these resources will evolve with you.

Invest time in your professional development, engage with your peers in the procurement community, and embrace innovation. The future of procurement is dynamic, and by mastering the tools and frameworks in these appendices, you will be well-equipped to drive long-term value and success for your organization.

Printed in Great Britain
by Amazon

61971310R00107

From Tactical to Strategic

Mastering the Art of Strategic Procurement Management

"Strategic procurement transcends mere transactions; it's about forging partnerships that drive innovation and deliver enduring value."